Collins

11+

Verbal Reasoning Comprehension

Support & Practice Workbook

Chris Pearse, Louise Swann,
Hilary Male and Lauren Pusey

Published by Collins
An imprint of HarperCollins*Publishers* Ltd
1 London Bridge Street
London SE1 9GF

HarperCollins*Publishers*
1st Floor, Watermarque Building, Ringsend Road, Dublin 4, Ireland

ISBN 978-0-00-849738-5

First published 2021

10 9 8 7 6 5 4 3 2 1

British Library Cataloguing in Publication Data.
A CIP record of this book is available from the British Library.
Commissioning: Clare Souza
Authors: Chris Pearse, Louise Swann, Hilary Male and Lauren Pusey
Project Management: Richard Toms and Sundus Pasha
Cover Design: Kevin Robbins and Sarah Duxbury
Inside Concept Design: Ian Wrigley
Typesetting and artwork: Jouve India Private Limited
Production: Karen Nulty

Published in collaboration with Teachitright.
Billy the Bookworm™ is the property of Teachitright Ltd.

Printed in the United Kingdom.

Contents

Contents

Introduction

Teachitright

This book has been published in collaboration with Teachitright, one of the most successful 11+ tuition companies in the South-East. It has supported thousands of pupils for both grammar school and independent school entry. Teachitright has several tuition centres across Berkshire, Buckinghamshire and West Midlands

With considerable experience and knowledge, Teachitright has produced a range of books to support children through their 11+ journey for both CEM style and many Common Entrance exams. The books have been written by qualified teachers, tested in the classroom with pupils and adapted to ensure children are fully prepared and able to perform to the best of their ability.

Teachitright's unique mascot, Billy, helps to guide children through this book and gives helpful hints and tips along the way. We hope your child finds this book useful and informative and we wish them luck on their 11+ journey.

Teachitright hold a number of comprehensive revision courses and mock exams throughout the year. For more information, please visit www.teachitright.com

Helping to build your child's future

How to use this book

This book uses a variety of different types of questions and these are outlined in the table below.

Type of question	How to locate the answer
Factual questions	These questions require the answer to be extracted directly from the text.
Inference questions	The answer will not be stated directly in the passage but can be solved by using clues in the extract. This involves reading between the lines.
Personal opinion questions	Using evidence in the extract, you can form a personal judgement and opinion about the text.
Grammar, literary devices and vocabulary questions	Knowledge of grammar and literary devices (e.g. alliteration), and a wide vocabulary base are needed to answer these questions. The answers will not be stated directly in the text.

Use the 5 steps below to work through each comprehension exercise:

(1) Read the passage first and try to comprehend what the text is saying.

(2) Do not skim-read as you might miss important parts and often links between the concepts need to be made.

(3) Underlining keywords or phrases can help you understand the passage and retain the important points. Do not underline everything in the extract as this might slow you down.

(4) After thoroughly reading the text, move on to the questions and refer back to the text to help you discover the answers. If given, use the line references to help you refer back to the relevant places in the passage.

(5) Double check you have answered all the questions and, if time allows, go back and read the passage for a second time.

Useful comprehension tips and hints

Billy will provide useful hints and tips throughout this book. Read these carefully before tackling the comprehensions as they can help improve your skills.

All the questions in this comprehension book are multiple choice and a horizontal line is used to show all the answers.

The **right** way to mark your answers on the answer sheet	The **wrong** way to mark your answers on the answer sheet
is the **right** way	is the **wrong** way
	is the **wrong** way
	is the **wrong** way
	is the **wrong** way

Billy's Vocabulary Pages

Billy the bookworm is here again to provide some fun activities after every comprehension. These additional pages will help you enhance your vocabulary and build on the skills already acquired during the comprehension exercise. The answers for these exciting pages are given at the back of the book in the 'Answers' section.

Mark scheme and recording results

The answers for all the comprehension questions are at the back of the book in the 'Answers' section. Each answer provides the correct letter choice and a detailed explanation on how each question can be solved.

To help you keep a track of your progress a 'Marking chart' on page 164 is provided at the back of the book for each comprehension. A 'Progress grid' on page 165 can be shaded in to help you to see your progress and keep a record of the results achieved. A series of statements are written on page 166 to help you identify the next steps.

Online video tutorial

An online video tutorial to help with techniques is available at www.collins.co.uk/11plusresources

SECTION 1:
COMPREHENSIONS

Look out for Billy's tips and hints.

1. ALICE IN WONDERLAND

Alice has found herself in the home of the Duchess who has a remarkable baby.

1 "Here! You may nurse it a bit, if you like!" the Duchess said to Alice, flinging the baby at her as she spoke. "I must go and get ready to play croquet with the Queen," and she hurried out of the room. The cook threw a frying-pan after her as she went out, but it just missed her.

5 Alice caught the baby with some difficulty, as it was a queer-shaped little creature, and held out its arms and legs in all directions, "just like a starfish," thought Alice. The poor little thing was snorting like a steam-engine when she caught it, and kept doubling itself up and straightening itself out again, so that altogether, for the first minute or two, it was as much as she could do to hold it.

10 As soon as she had made out the proper way of nursing it (which was to twist it up into a sort of knot, and then keep tight hold of its right ear and left foot, so as to prevent its undoing itself), she carried it out into the open air. "If I don't take this child away with me," thought Alice, "they're sure to kill it in a day or two: wouldn't it be murder to leave it behind?" She said the last words out loud, and the little thing grunted in reply (it had
15 left off sneezing by this time). "Don't grunt," said Alice, "that's not at all a proper way of expressing yourself."

The baby grunted again, and Alice looked very anxiously into its face to see what was the matter with it. There could be no doubt that it had a very turn-up nose, much more like a snout than a real nose; also its eyes were getting extremely small for a
20 baby: altogether Alice did not like the look of the thing at all. "But perhaps it was only sobbing," she thought, and looked into its eyes again, to see if there were any tears.

No, there were no tears. "If you're going to turn into a pig, my dear," said Alice, seriously, "I'll have nothing more to do with you. Mind now!" The poor little thing sobbed again (or grunted, it was impossible to say which), and they went on for some while in
25 silence. Alice was just beginning to think to herself, "Now, what am I to do with this creature when I get it home?", when it grunted again, so violently, that she looked down into its face in some alarm. This time there could be no mistake about it: it was neither more nor less than a pig, and she felt that it would be quite absurd for her to carry it further. So she set the little creature down, and felt quite relieved to see it trot away
30 quietly into the wood. "If it had grown up," she said to herself, "it would have made a dreadfully ugly child: but it makes rather a handsome pig, I think." And she began thinking over other children she knew, who might do very well as pigs, and was just saying to herself, "If one only knew the right way to change them", when she was a little startled by seeing the Cheshire Cat sitting on a bough of a tree a few yards off.

35 The Cat only grinned when it saw Alice. It looked good-natured, she thought: still it had very long claws and a great many teeth, so she felt that it ought to be treated with respect.

"Cheshire Puss," she began, rather timidly, as she did not at all know whether it would like the name: however, it only grinned a little wider. "Come, it's pleased so far," thought
40 Alice, and she went on. "Would you tell me, please, which way I ought to go from here?"

"That depends a good deal on where you want to get to," said the Cat.

"I don't much care where—" said Alice.

"Then it doesn't matter which way you go," said the Cat.

"—so long as I get somewhere," Alice added as an explanation.

45 "Oh, you're sure to do that," said the Cat, "if you only walk long enough."

1. ALICE IN WONDERLAND questions

(1) Why did the Duchess give Alice the baby to nurse?
- [ ] **A** She was afraid the cook would hurt the baby.
- [ ] **B** She wanted to go and get ready for a game of croquet.
- [ ] **C** She was in a hurry to leave the room.
- [ ] **D** She couldn't keep hold of the baby's arms and legs.
- [ ] **E** The Queen had ordered her to leave the room at once.

(2) "The poor little thing was snorting like a steam engine". (lines 6–7)
Which of the following literary devices are used here?
i. onomatopoeia　　ii. simile　　iii. personification　　iv. alliteration
- [ ] **A** 1 and 2
- [ ] **B** 2 and 4
- [ ] **C** 2 and 3
- [ ] **D** 3 and 4
- [ ] **E** All of the above

(3) Why did Alice "set the little creature down"? (line 29)
- [ ] **A** She didn't want any more to do with the little creature.
- [ ] **B** The creature was wriggling too much for her to hold it.
- [ ] **C** It was so obviously a pig, it would be ridiculous to treat it as a baby.
- [ ] **D** The creature was making too much noise.
- [ ] **E** It was too ugly for her to believe it was a baby any more.

(4) How did Alice feel as she carried the baby into the open air?
- [ ] **A** Angry that the Duchess had thrown the baby at her
- [ ] **B** Confused as to how to hold the baby
- [ ] **C** Disinterested in what was happening to the baby
- [ ] **D** Excited to have a baby to care for
- [ ] **E** Worried that she would be responsible for the baby's death if she didn't take it away

(5) Why did Alice describe the baby as "just like a starfish"? (line 6)
- [ ] **A** Its limbs were protruding everywhere.
- [ ] **B** It sounded like a starfish.
- [ ] **C** Alice wasn't sure what the baby was turning into.
- [ ] **D** The cook had been preparing fish.
- [ ] **E** The baby was slippery like a starfish.

(6) What is the best synonym for "flinging"? (line 1)
- [ ] **A** Dancing
- [ ] **B** Shooting
- [ ] **C** Flying
- [ ] **D** Throwing
- [ ] **E** Rolling

7. Why did Alice go to the home of the Duchess?
   - [ ] **A** To look after the baby
   - [ ] **B** To meet the Duchess
   - [ ] **C** To play croquet
   - [ ] **D** To find out how to get back home
   - [ ] **E** The text doesn't say

8. What is the meaning of the phrase "neither more nor less than a pig"? (lines 27–28)
   - [ ] **A** The baby was more like a pig than before.
   - [ ] **B** The baby was less like a pig than it had been.
   - [ ] **C** The baby had completed its transformation into a pig.
   - [ ] **D** Alice wasn't sure what was happening to the baby.
   - [ ] **E** It was no longer a baby or a pig

9. "Alice did not like the look of the thing at all"? (line 20)
   Which part of this sentence is the object of the sentence?
   - [ ] **A** The thing
   - [ ] **B** Alice
   - [ ] **C** The look
   - [ ] **D** Like
   - [ ] **E** At all

10. Why did she look into the baby's eyes? (line 21)
    - [ ] **A** She was anxious to find out what the matter was.
    - [ ] **B** She wanted to see if its eyes were getting smaller.
    - [ ] **C** She was wondering why the baby was sneezing.
    - [ ] **D** She was looking for evidence that the creature was human.
    - [ ] **E** The baby's eyes had changed colour.

11. Which of the following best describes Alice's encounter with the baby?
    1. Humorous
    2. Shocking
    3. Realistic
    4. Fantasy
    - [ ] **A** 1 and 2
    - [ ] **B** 1 and 4
    - [ ] **C** 2 and 3
    - [ ] **D** 1 and 3
    - [ ] **E** 3 and 4

12. What was Alice's opinion of the pig as she watched it trot into the wood?
    - [ ] **A** She was fed up with nursing it.
    - [ ] **B** She thought it had become a good looking pig.
    - [ ] **C** She was pleased to see the back of the creature.
    - [ ] **D** She wanted to go home.
    - [ ] **E** She had noticed the Cheshire Cat.

(13) Where did Alice see the Cheshire Cat?

- [ ] **A** Sitting on the path
- [ ] **B** Curled up in a hollow tree
- [ ] **C** Among the leaves of a bush
- [ ] **D** Perched on the branch of a tree
- [ ] **E** Grinning on a tree stump

(14) Why did Alice feel timid when she spoke to the cat?

- [ ] **A** She was afraid of his long claws.
- [ ] **B** She didn't know if he would understand her.
- [ ] **C** She found that the cat was good natured.
- [ ] **D** She felt she should treat it with respect.
- [ ] **E** She wasn't sure the cat would like what she called it.

(15) What is the best definition for "handsome"? (line 31)

- [ ] **A** Nimble
- [ ] **B** Good looking
- [ ] **C** Large
- [ ] **D** Well-dressed
- [ ] **E** Four legged

(16) What did Alice want to find out from the cat?

- [ ] **A** How far was the rabbit hole
- [ ] **B** Where the pig was going
- [ ] **C** Whether the cat was pleased with her
- [ ] **D** Which direction she should travel in next
- [ ] **E** How he had appeared in the tree

(17) What is the best antonym for the word "pleased"? (line 39)

- [ ] **A** Thank you
- [ ] **B** Contented
- [ ] **C** Dissatisfied
- [ ] **D** Unhelpful
- [ ] **E** Depressed

(18) Where does most of the action take place in this part of the story?

- [ ] **A** In a dark wood near a path
- [ ] **B** Beside a path under a tree
- [ ] **C** Under a tree near a house
- [ ] **D** Outside a house by a wood
- [ ] **E** In a house under a tree

(19) What type of writing is this passage?

- [ ] **A** First person narrative
- [ ] **B** First person report
- [ ] **C** Third person narrative
- [ ] **D** Third person report
- [ ] **E** None of the above

20. Who do you think this passage was originally intended for?
- ☐ **A** Children
- ☐ **B** Babies
- ☐ **C** Teenagers
- ☐ **D** Adults
- ☐ **E** Elderly people

Remember, evidence for all answers is always in the text!

BILLY'S PERFECT PRONOUNS

Throughout *Alice in Wonderland*, there are lots of pronouns. Pronouns are used to replace either a proper noun or a common noun.

Can you fill in the blanks in the sentences below with the correct pronoun from the passage?

She	her	you
I	herself	yourself

1) _____ must go and get ready to play croquet with the Queen.

2) "Would _____ tell me, please, which way I ought to go from here?"

3) _____ said the last words out loud, and the little thing grunted in reply.

4) "That's not at all a proper way of expressing _____."

5) Alice was just beginning to think to _____, "Now what am I to do with this creature when I get it home?"

6) The cook threw a frying-pan after her as she went out, but it just missed _____.

   Can you find any more pronouns used in the passage? Write them below.

   _____

We use pronouns so that we don't need to keep repeating the same noun.

2. DRAGONS

Who doesn't enjoy a story which includes a dragon? They have appeared in stories which have for centuries simultaneously frightened and delighted children of all ages.

1 A dragon is a mythical beast which features in the myths of many cultures. There are two distinct types of dragon. European folklore envisages a dragon as a giant reptilian creature with scales or feathers and invariably winged. They are depicted as having enormous claws and teeth and the awesome ability to spew fire. Conversely, Chinese

5 dragons resemble large snakes and are wingless quadrupeds. They, unlike their malevolent European counterparts who possess only animal intelligence, are associated with wisdom and supernatural powers and are revered as very intelligent representatives of the primal forces of nature, religion and the universe. A dragon is the only mythical creature included in the twelve animals which represent the Chinese calendar. This is a powerful indicator

10 of its supremacy in the Chinese animal hierarchy, above even the mighty tiger, powerful horse and the sneaky rat.

Traditional narratives about dragons often involve a hero slaying a dragon, the catalyst for such violence being the predilection of dragons to consume damsels, demolish villages and keep huge hordes of shiny treasure which attract and inspire both the brave and the

15 avaricious to heroic feats of endurance. 'St George and the Dragon' is probably the most famous of these stories. There are many versions of this tale but most concur on the terrorisation of a village, the proposed sacrifice of a princess and the rescue of her by St George.

My favourite dragon is Smaug who features in Tolkein's fantastic story, *The Hobbit*. He is

20 portrayed as a supremely violent, cruel and intelligent character with an unquenchable thirst for gold. However, his most distinguishing characteristic (apart from his greed) is his arrogance. His reddish-gold scales render him impervious to nearly all weapons but his soft underbelly is vulnerable. Ingeniously Smaug sleeps on a bed of gold and jewels which embed in his body and make a "diamond waistcoat", which gives him almost complete

25 protection. Only his boasting finally seals his doom. Smaug is a complex character and I have always felt a surprising affection for him.

Another story which I enjoy is 'There's No Such Thing as a Dragon' by Jack Kent. In this story, simple on the surface, bigger ideas are expounded. It seems to me to be an allegorical tale which explores the idea that a little bit of attention can make

30 a big difference. The cute little dragon simply wants to be noticed and, by making a traditionally tyrannical creature so loveable and defenceless, the author makes his point powerfully. For me, it finally dispelled that old adage "children should be seen and not heard". You should read it!

Nowadays the popular computer game 'Dungeons and Dragons' makes heavy use of

35 dragons. Though dragons usually serve as adversaries, they are not always so. Their

alignment is determined by their species. For example, a red dragon breathes fire and is evil while a silver dragon is good and breathes gold. I have been told that these games are great fun although I am neither familiar with nor interested in them.

40 Although dragons are mythical beasts, they are occasionally inclined to metamorphose into human form. I can be certain of this because only recently I overheard a pupil whom I know to be quite fond of me, whisper into her friend's ear, "She's a right dragon today." Clearly I can, on occasion, be more formidable than I thought!

When answering the multiple-choice questions, first eliminate the wrong answers to help limit your options.

2. DRAGONS questions

① How are dragons regarded in Chinese culture?
- [ ] **A** With indifference
- [ ] **B** With respect
- [ ] **C** With interest
- [ ] **D** With fear
- [ ] **E** With affection

② The author believes dragon stories can be enjoyed by:
- [ ] **A** Only adults
- [ ] **B** Only children
- [ ] **C** Everyone
- [ ] **D** Nobody
- [ ] **E** Only boys

③ "She's a right dragon today" is an example of:
- [ ] **A** A proverb
- [ ] **B** A simile
- [ ] **C** A metaphor
- [ ] **D** Personification
- [ ] **E** Assonance

④ "Children should be seen and not heard" means:
- [ ] **A** Children should be gagged.
- [ ] **B** People should not look at or listen to children.
- [ ] **C** Children should never speak.
- [ ] **D** Children should behave well and be quiet in adult company.
- [ ] **E** Children should be decorative.

⑤ When the author states that dragons can sometimes change into humans, she intends to be:
- [ ] **A** Sarcastic
- [ ] **B** Modest
- [ ] **C** Ironic
- [ ] **D** Boastful
- [ ] **E** Honest

⑥ According to the text, which two of these statements are true?
1. All dragons have wings.
2. All dragons look like lizards.
3. Some dragons can breathe fire.
4. Dragons can vary in intelligence.
5. All dragons have scales.

	A	Statement 1 and 2
	B	Statement 2 and 4
	C	Statement 2 and 3
	D	Statement 3 and 5
	E	Statement 3 and 4

⑦ The word "envisages" (line 2) is synonymous with:

	A	Imagines
	B	Sketches
	C	Expects
	D	Disregards
	E	Understands

⑧ The word "conversely" (line 4) in an example of:

	A	A noun
	B	A verb
	C	An adverb
	D	A preposition
	E	An adjective

⑨ Which of these characteristics is most dominant in the personality of Smaug?

	A	Modesty
	B	Cruelty
	C	Arrogance
	D	Greed
	E	Sense of humour

⑩ The most likely place for Smaug to receive a mortal injury would be in:

	A	His eye
	B	His head
	C	His stomach
	D	His tail
	E	His foot

⑪ Why do you think the author is surprised by her affection for Smaug?

	A	Smaug has few pleasant attributes.
	B	She likes cruel characters.
	C	She doesn't like intelligent characters.
	D	She doesn't usually like cuddly toys.
	E	Smaug is ugly.

⑫ The author thinks that Jack Kent's use of a dragon as a character is:

	A	Stupid
	B	Amusing
	C	Spiteful
	D	Cunning
	E	Clever

13 'Dungeons and Dragons' uses dragons:

- [ ] **A** Occasionally
- [ ] **B** Repeatedly
- [ ] **C** Rarely
- [ ] **D** Never
- [ ] **E** Sporadically

14 What sort of teacher do you think the author would be?

- [ ] **A** Always very strict
- [ ] **B** Never humorous
- [ ] **C** Always kind and gentle
- [ ] **D** Firm but fair
- [ ] **E** Inept

15 According to the text, children find stories about dragons:

- [ ] **A** Terrifying
- [ ] **B** Amazing
- [ ] **C** Pleasurable
- [ ] **D** None of the above
- [ ] **E** All of the above

16 An antonym for the word "malevolent" is:

- [ ] **A** Beneficiary
- [ ] **B** Belligerent
- [ ] **C** Benevolent
- [ ] **D** Bespeckled
- [ ] **E** Behind

17 Which character is the most important in the Chinese animal hierarchy?

- [ ] **A** The mighty tiger
- [ ] **B** The sneaky rat
- [ ] **C** The powerful horse
- [ ] **D** The dragon
- [ ] **E** The clever mouse

18 What motive apart from the desire to be brave does the author think causes a protagonist to steal from a dragon?

- [ ] **A** Greed
- [ ] **B** Poverty
- [ ] **C** Stupidity
- [ ] **D** Honour
- [ ] **E** Aggression

19 'There's No Such Thing as a Dragon' is a story that the author thinks you would:
- A   Dislike
- B   Not understand
- C   Benefit from reading
- D   Find suitable for adults
- E   Be bored by

20 Which word do you think would accurately describe the author's attitude towards 'Dungeons and Dragons'?
- A   Ignorant
- B   Indifferent
- C   Enthusiastic
- D   Loathing
- E   Amused

Always read the whole passage carefully so you don't miss any important details. Only skim and scan when you start answering the questions.

BILLY'S AMAZING ADJECTIVES

How many adjectives can you find in the passage to describe dragons? Write them round the dragon.

Use the scale below to rate your adjective hunting skills!

0–5	Ok
6–10	Average
11–15	Good
16–20	Very good
21+	Wow!

Refer to page 136 for answers.

Adjectives describe things, people or places. Using adjectives in your writing makes it more interesting for the reader.

3. WEATHERS

1 This is the weather the cuckoo likes,
    And so do I;
    When showers betumble the chestnut spikes,
    And nestlings fly;
5 And the little brown nightingale bills his best,
    And they sit outside at "The Traveller's Rest,"
    And maids come forth sprig-muslin drest,
    And citizens dream of the south and west,
    And so do I.

10 This is the weather the shepherd shuns,
    And so do I;
    When beeches drip in browns and duns,
    And thresh and ply;
    And hill-hid tides throb, throe on throe,
15 And meadow rivulets overflow,
    And drops on gate bars hang in a row,
    And rooks in families homeward go,
    And so do I.

by Thomas Hardy

3. WEATHERS questions

1. At what time of the year is the first verse set?
   - ☐ **A** Christmas
   - ☐ **B** Early summer
   - ☐ **C** Early autumn
   - ☐ **D** Winter
   - ☐ **E** It is not inferred in the poem

2. What does the rain do? (line 3)
   - ☐ **A** Knocks the chestnut blossom over
   - ☐ **B** Falls heavily on to the trees
   - ☐ **C** Knocks the chestnut trees down
   - ☐ **D** Allows the sharp shoots of chestnuts to grow
   - ☐ **E** Makes cuckoos fly home

3. What is the best description of a "nestling"? (line 4)
   - ☐ **A** A bird building a nest
   - ☐ **B** A baby bird in its nest
   - ☐ **C** A cuckoo in a nest
   - ☐ **D** A mother bird bringing food to its young
   - ☐ **E** A bird flying to its nest

4. "The little brown nightingale bills his best." (line 5)
   What literary feature is used here?
   - ☐ **A** Personification
   - ☐ **B** A simile
   - ☐ **C** A metaphor
   - ☐ **D** Onamatopoeia
   - ☐ **E** Alliteration

5. What do you think Thomas Hardy means by "The Traveller's Rest"? (line 6)
   - ☐ **A** A place where you can have a rest after a journey
   - ☐ **B** A bus stop
   - ☐ **C** A railway station
   - ☐ **D** The name of a pub
   - ☐ **E** Somewhere you can meet the rest of the travellers

6. In which person and tense is the poem written?
   - ☐ **A** Third person, present tense
   - ☐ **B** First person, present tense
   - ☐ **C** First person, past tense
   - ☐ **D** Third person, past tense
   - ☐ **E** Poem does not make this clear

⑦ What do the young girls do at this time of year?

- [ ] **A** Listen to cuckoos
- [ ] **B** Relax and sit outside in the sun
- [ ] **C** Go out wearing flowery dresses
- [ ] **D** Watch baby birds
- [ ] **E** Go on their travels

⑧ What is the best definition of the word "citizens"? (line 8)

- [ ] **A** The inhabitants of a country
- [ ] **B** Children on holiday
- [ ] **C** Young girls
- [ ] **D** People living in the city
- [ ] **E** Nature lovers

⑨ Why do the citizens "dream of the south and west"? (line 8)

- [ ] **A** They are sleeping in the sun.
- [ ] **B** They are looking forward to going on holiday.
- [ ] **C** They want to go and live somewhere warmer.
- [ ] **D** They are tired from all their work.
- [ ] **E** The birds are going to fly south.

⑩ Which would the best modern spelling for "drest"? (line 7)

- [ ] **A** Dress
- [ ] **B** Dread
- [ ] **C** Dance
- [ ] **D** Dressed
- [ ] **E** Dresser

⑪ Which is the best synonym for the word "shuns"? (line 10)

- [ ] **A** Dislikes
- [ ] **B** Desires
- [ ] **C** Avoids
- [ ] **D** Ignores
- [ ] **E** Fears

⑫ What do you think the word "bills" means?

- [ ] **A** Builds
- [ ] **B** Listens
- [ ] **C** Sings
- [ ] **D** Eats
- [ ] **E** Pecks

13   Why do the "beeches drip in browns and duns"? (line 12)

- [ ] **A**   The trees are losing their leaves
- [ ] **B**   Because the rain is falling at the seaside making everything wet and colourless
- [ ] **C**   Because bad weather has spoiled everyone's holiday
- [ ] **D**   Because the heavy rain is running from the dark trees
- [ ] **E**   Because in the winter there are no green leaves

14   Most of the lines of this poem begin with "And". Why do you think Thomas Hardy does this?

1.   It enhances rhythm within the poem.
2.   It helps the poem to rhyme
3.   It builds on the picture of all the things which happen in each type of weather.
4.   It is a grammatical error.

- [ ] **A**   1 and 3
- [ ] **B**   1 and 2
- [ ] **C**   3 and 4
- [ ] **D**   2 and 3
- [ ] **E**   All four

15   How does the poet describe the gates in bad weather?

- [ ] **A**   They have water hanging along them in drops.
- [ ] **B**   They are brown and without colour.
- [ ] **C**   They are open to let the poet pass by.
- [ ] **D**   They are standing in a flooded lane.
- [ ] **E**   They are difficult to get through.

16   What has happened to the little streams in the second verse?

- [ ] **A**   They have dried up.
- [ ] **B**   They are hidden behind hills.
- [ ] **C**   They are flooding onto the meadows.
- [ ] **D**   They are watched carefully by the poet.
- [ ] **E**   They are deep and dark.

17   What part of speech is the word "rooks" in line 17?

- [ ] **A**   Abstract noun
- [ ] **B**   Proper noun
- [ ] **C**   Collective noun
- [ ] **D**   Plural common noun
- [ ] **E**   Adjective

18   What do the rooks have in common with the poet?

- [ ] **A**   They like bad weather.
- [ ] **B**   They live in nests.
- [ ] **C**   They enjoy the countryside.
- [ ] **D**   They watch the seasons come and go.
- [ ] **E**   They head for home in bad weather.

19 Why does Thomas Hardy feel differently about rain in the first and second verses?

- ☐ **A** There is too much rain in the first verse.
- ☐ **B** It is far too dry in the first verse.
- ☐ **C** It is pleasant to have a shower when it's hot but too much rain is uncomfortable.
- ☐ **D** Rain does damage to trees in the spring.
- ☐ **E** He dislikes rain in both seasons.

20 Which word best describes the weather in the first verse?

- ☐ **A** Mild
- ☐ **B** Inclement
- ☐ **C** Harsh
- ☐ **D** Overcast
- ☐ **E** Violent

While answering the comprehension questions, always refer back to the passage to clarify your answer.

BILLY'S ROBUST RHYMES

The poem 'Weathers' is written using rhyme. The rhyming words are found at the end of the lines:

> And the little brown nightingale bills his best,
> And they sit outside at 'The Traveller's Rest'

Rhyming words are words that sound the same when spoken, but they don't necessarily have to be spelt the same.

Can you find 5 more pairs of rhyming words in 'Weathers'?

_____ _____

_____ _____

_____ _____

_____ _____

_____ _____

Try writing a poem using a rhyme.

_____

_____

_____

_____

Shakespeare used rhyming couplets to end a scene or a play: 'For never was a story of more woe, Than this of Juliet and her Romeo.'

4. THE MERCHANT OF VENICE

'Portia arrives in her disguise to defend Antonio. Given the authority of judgment by the Duke, Portia decides that Shylock can have the pound of flesh as long as he doesn't draw blood, as it is against the law to shed a Christian's blood. Since it is obvious that to draw a pound of flesh would kill Antonio, Shylock is denied his suit. Moreover, for conspiring to murder a Venetian citizen, Portia orders that he should forfeit all his wealth. Half is to go to Venice, and half to Antonio.'

Portia:

1 The quality of mercy is not strained.
    It droppeth as the gentle rain from heaven
    Upon the place beneath. It is twice blessed:
    It blesseth him that gives and him that takes.
5 'Tis mightiest in the mightiest. It becomes
    The throned monarch better than his crown.
    His sceptre shows the force of temporal power,
    The attribute to awe and majesty
    Wherein doth sit the dread and fear of kings,
10 But mercy is above this sceptred sway
    It is enthroned in the hearts of kings.
    It is an attribute to God himself.
    And earthly power doth then show likest God's
    When mercy seasons justice. Therefore, Jew
15 Though justice be thy plea, consider this –
    That in the course of justice none of us
    Should see salvation. We do pray for mercy.
    And that same prayer doth teach us all to render
    The deeds of mercy. I have spoken thus much
20 To mitigate the justice of thy plea,
    Which if thou follow, this strict court of Venice
    Must needs give sentence 'gainst the merchant there.

Shylock:

    My deeds upon head. I crave the law,
    The penalty and forfeit of my bond.

Portia:

25 Tarry a little. There is something else.
    This bond doth give thee here no jot of blood.
    The words expressly are 'a pound of flesh'.
    Take then thy bond, take thou thy pound of flesh,
    But in the cutting if it thou dost shed
30 One drop of Christian blood, thy lands and goods
    Are by the laws of Venice confiscate.
    Unto the state of Venice.

4. THE MERCHANT OF VENICE questions

1. "It droppeth as the gentle rain from heaven" is an example of:
   - [ ] **A** A metaphor
   - [ ] **B** Personification
   - [ ] **C** A simile
   - [ ] **D** Alliteration
   - [ ] **E** A proverb

2. The word "mercy" is: (line 1)
   - [ ] **A** A common noun
   - [ ] **B** A proper noun
   - [ ] **C** An abstract noun
   - [ ] **D** An adjective
   - [ ] **E** An adverb

3. "'Tis" can be expanded to make: (line 5)
   - [ ] **A** A pronoun and a verb
   - [ ] **B** A noun
   - [ ] **C** A pronoun
   - [ ] **D** A preposition
   - [ ] **E** A noun and a verb

4. Which of the following words is closest in meaning to the word "strict"? (line 21)
   - [ ] **A** Stern
   - [ ] **B** Kind
   - [ ] **C** Scary
   - [ ] **D** Harshly
   - [ ] **E** Just

5. Which of the following words is closest in meaning to "strained"? (line 1)
   - [ ] **A** Wanted
   - [ ] **B** Filtered
   - [ ] **C** Needed
   - [ ] **D** Pleasant
   - [ ] **E** Forced

6. To whom or to what does "It" refer? (line 4)
   - [ ] **A** The giver and receiver
   - [ ] **B** The weather
   - [ ] **C** The King
   - [ ] **D** A sneeze
   - [ ] **E** Mercy

7. The quality of mercy makes a king look better than:
   - [ ] **A** His crown
   - [ ] **B** His sceptre
   - [ ] **C** His clothes
   - [ ] **D** His throne
   - [ ] **E** God

8. According to the text, a king's sceptre is:
   - [ ] **A** A symbol of a king's power and authority
   - [ ] **B** Something that we should be afraid of
   - [ ] **C** Something that the king's is afraid of
   - [ ] **D** Like a magic wand
   - [ ] **E** A weapon

9. According to the text, the heart of a good king contains:
   - [ ] **A** Mercy
   - [ ] **B** Truth
   - [ ] **C** Hatred
   - [ ] **D** Forgiveness
   - [ ] **E** Weakness

10. According to the text, God is:
    - [ ] **A** Angry
    - [ ] **B** Proud
    - [ ] **C** Compassionate
    - [ ] **D** Jealous
    - [ ] **E** Cruel

11. According to the text, a king is most like God when he:
    - [ ] **A** Holds his sceptre
    - [ ] **B** Puts salt on his food
    - [ ] **C** Is fair to everyone
    - [ ] **D** Shows his power
    - [ ] **E** Mixes mercy with justice

12. What does Portia think that we ask God for in our prayers?
    - [ ] **A** Salvation
    - [ ] **B** Justice
    - [ ] **C** Money
    - [ ] **D** Mercy
    - [ ] **E** Honesty

13. Portia says (line 18) that we should all "render" (which means "give") mercy to other people. In your opinion, why does she think that we should do this?
    - [ ] **A** Because she is in charge
    - [ ] **B** Because it will make us rich
    - [ ] **C** Because we should give what we expect to be given
    - [ ] **D** Because then we will not have to pay for it ourselves
    - [ ] **E** Because we should be kind

(14) What do you think Portia is trying to make Shylock feel?
- ☐ **A** Sad
- ☐ **B** Angry
- ☐ **C** Ashamed
- ☐ **D** Amused
- ☐ **E** More determined

(15) If Shylock insists on justice, Antonio will:
- ☐ **A** Go free
- ☐ **B** Chase Shylock away
- ☐ **C** Be forced to give the pound of flesh
- ☐ **D** Get married
- ☐ **E** Be grateful

(16) As Shylock prepares to cut, Portia tells him that he must: (line 25)
- ☐ **A** Be gentle
- ☐ **B** Sharpen his knife
- ☐ **C** Think some more
- ☐ **D** Wait a moment
- ☐ **E** Say a prayer

(17) Portia forbids Shylock to take:
- ☐ **A** More than one pound of flesh
- ☐ **B** More than one drop of blood
- ☐ **C** Even one drop of blood
- ☐ **D** Plenty of time
- ☐ **E** Antonio's land

(18) Which word best describes Portia as she appears in the extract?
- ☐ **A** Upset
- ☐ **B** Mean
- ☐ **C** Funny
- ☐ **D** Deceitful
- ☐ **E** Clever

(19) If Shylock breaks the law, Portia determines to:
- ☐ **A** Put him in prison
- ☐ **B** Banish him to Venice
- ☐ **C** Take all his land, property and money
- ☐ **D** Have him thrown in jail
- ☐ **E** Have him executed

(20) How do you think Shylock will react to Portia's conditions?
- ☐ **A** He will apologise.
- ☐ **B** He will marry Portia.
- ☐ **C** He will leave quietly.
- ☐ **D** He will be very angry.
- ☐ **E** He will see the funny side.

BILLY'S SYNONYMOUS SHAKESPEARE

Below is *The Merchant of Venice* extract changed into a modern text. Can you discover the Shakespearian word for the ones highlighted?

Portia:

No one shows mercy because he has to. It just happens, the way gentle rain drops on the ground. Mercy is a double blessing. It blesses the one who gives it and the one who receives it. It's strongest in the strongest people. It looks better in a king than his own crown looks on him. The king's sceptre represents his earthly power, the symbol of majesty, the focus of royal authority. But mercy is higher than the sceptre. It's enthroned in the hearts of kings, a quality of God himself. Kingly power seems most like God's power when the king mixes mercy with justice. So although justice is your plea, consider this. Justice won't save our souls. We pray for mercy, and this same prayer teaches us to show mercy to others as well. I've told you this to make you give up this case. If you pursue it, this strict court of Venice will need to carry out the sentence against the merchant there.

Shylock:

I take all responsibility for my decisions. I want the law, the penalty, and the fulfilment of my contract.

Portia:

But wait a moment. There's something else. This contract doesn't give you any blood at all. The words expressly specify "a pound of flesh". So take your penalty of a pound of flesh but, if you shed one drop of blood when you cut it, the state of Venice will confiscate your land and property under Venetian law.

1)	blesses	_____
2)	strongest	_____
3)	the focus of	_____
4)	give	_____
5)	you	_____
6)	pursue	_____
7)	decisions	_____
8)	carry out	_____
9)	But wait a moment	_____
10)	your	_____

Try acting out *The Merchant of Venice* play script with a friend as this will really develop your characterisation!

5. TREASURE ISLAND

Jim is a cabin boy on a ship which is searching for treasure. Having covertly witnessed Long John Silver (the ship's cook) committing murder, he decides to flee onto an island. On the island, he encounters a half-crazed Englishman.

1 From the side of the hill, which was here steep and stony, a spout of gravel was dislodged and fell rattling and bounding through the trees. My eyes turned instinctively in that direction, and I saw a figure leap with great rapidity behind the trunk of a pine. What it was, whether bear or man or monkey, I could in no wise tell. It seemed dark and shaggy;

5 more I knew not. But the terror of this new apparition brought me to a stand. I was now, it seemed, cut off upon both sides; behind me the murderers, before me this lurking nondescript. And immediately I began to prefer the dangers that I knew to those I knew not. Silver himself appeared less terrible in contrast with this creature of the woods, and I turned on my heel, and looking sharply behind me over my shoulder, began to retrace

10 my steps in the direction of the boats.

Instantly the figure reappeared, and making a wide circuit, began to head me off. I was tired, at any rate; but had I been as fresh as when I rose, I could see it was in vain for me to contend in speed with such an adversary. From trunk to trunk the creature flitted like a deer, running manlike on two legs, but unlike any man that I had ever seen, stooping

15 almost double as it ran. Yet a man it was, I could no longer be in doubt about that. I began to recall what I had heard of cannibals. I was within an ace of calling for help. But the mere fact that he was a man, however wild, had somewhat reassured me, and my fear of Silver began to revive in proportion. I stood still, therefore, and cast about for some method of escape; and as I was so thinking, the recollection of my pistol flashed

20 into my mind. As soon as I remembered I was not defenceless, courage glowed again in my heart and I set my face resolutely for this man of the island and walked briskly towards him.

He was concealed by this time behind another tree trunk; but he must have been watching me closely, for as soon as I began to move in his direction he reappeared and

25 took a step to meet me. Then he hesitated, drew back, came forward again, and at last, to my wonder and confusion, threw himself on his knees and held out his clasped hands in supplication.

At that I once more stopped.

"Who are you?" I asked.

30 "Ben Gunn," he answered, and his voice sounded hoarse and awkward, like a rusty lock.

"I'm poor Ben Gunn, I am; and I haven't spoke with a Christian these three years."

I could now see that he was a white man like myself and that his features were even pleasing. His skin, wherever it was exposed, was burnt by the sun; even his lips were black, and his fair eyes looked quite startling in so dark a face. Of all the beggar-men

35 that I had seen or fancied, he was the chief for raggedness. He was clothed with tatters of old ship's canvas and old sea-cloth, and this extraordinary patchwork was all held together by a system of the most various and incongruous fastenings, brass buttons, bits of stick, and loops of tarry gaskin. About his waist he wore an old brass-buckled leather belt, which was the one thing solid in his whole accoutrement.

40 "Three years!" I cried. "Were you shipwrecked?"

"Nay, mate," said he; "marooned."

I had heard the word, and I knew it stood for a horrible kind of punishment common enough among the buccaneers, in which the offender is put ashore with a little powder and shot and left behind on some desolate and distant island.

45 "Marooned three years agone," he continued, "and lived on goats since then, and berries, and oysters. Wherever a man is, says I, a man can do for himself. But, mate, my heart is sore for Christian diet. You mightn't happen to have a piece of cheese about you, now? No? Well, many's the long night I've dreamed of cheese—toasted, mostly—and woke up again, and here I were."

50 "If ever I can get aboard again," said I, "you shall have cheese by the stone."

All this time he had been feeling the stuff of my jacket, smoothing my hands, looking at my boots, and generally, in the intervals of his speech, showing a childish pleasure in the presence of a fellow creature. But at my last words he perked up into a kind of startled slyness.

55 "If ever you can get aboard again, says you?" he repeated. "Why, now, who's to hinder you?"

"Not you, I know," was my reply.

5. TREASURE ISLAND questions

① How did Ben Gunn first reveal his presence to Jim?
- ☐ **A** He shouted.
- ☐ **B** He whispered.
- ☐ **C** He caused a noise.
- ☐ **D** He coughed.
- ☐ **E** He threw stones.

② The word "spout" (line 1) in this context means:
- ☐ **A** Part of a teapot
- ☐ **B** A pile
- ☐ **C** To rant
- ☐ **D** A spurt
- ☐ **E** A gush of water

③ Jim could not immediately identify the figure as a man because:
- ☐ **A** He was disguised.
- ☐ **B** He was hiding behind a bush.
- ☐ **C** Jim was too far away.
- ☐ **D** Jim needed glasses.
- ☐ **E** The man disappeared too quickly.

④ Jim stopped still because:
- ☐ **A** He was frightened of falling over.
- ☐ **B** He was frightened that the stone would cut him.
- ☐ **C** He was afraid of the creature.
- ☐ **D** The road was blocked by gravel.
- ☐ **E** He had hurt his foot.

⑤ A synonym for the word "lurking" (line 6) would be:
- ☐ **A** Creeping
- ☐ **B** Skulking
- ☐ **C** Moaning
- ☐ **D** Scary
- ☐ **E** Anonymous

⑥ The word "manlike" (line 14) is:
- ☐ **A** An adjective
- ☐ **B** A noun
- ☐ **C** A simile
- ☐ **D** An adverb
- ☐ **E** A preposition

7. Jim goes back the way he came because:

- [ ] **A** He is more frightened of Silver than of the creature.
- [ ] **B** He is more frightened of the creature than of Silver.
- [ ] **C** He hopes to escape both.
- [ ] **D** He wants to look for the boat.
- [ ] **E** He forgot something.

8. (Line 13) "flitted like a deer" is an example of:

- [ ] **A** A simile
- [ ] **B** Onomatopoeia
- [ ] **C** A metaphor
- [ ] **D** An idiom
- [ ] **E** A proverb

9. Jim is afraid that the man might:

- [ ] **A** Shoot him
- [ ] **B** Cut off his head
- [ ] **C** Eat him
- [ ] **D** Help him
- [ ] **E** Tickle him

10. If Jim were to be attacked, what do you think he would most likely do?

- [ ] **A** Run away
- [ ] **B** Fight with his fists
- [ ] **C** Hide
- [ ] **D** Shoot them
- [ ] **E** Try to talk to them

11. Which of these words do you think would best describe Jim's character?

- [ ] **A** Brave and determined
- [ ] **B** Clever and innovative
- [ ] **C** Timid and scared
- [ ] **D** Cunning and duplicitous
- [ ] **E** Generous and kind

12. In your opinion, why does the man keep advancing and retreating towards Jim?

- [ ] **A** He is trying to confuse Jim.
- [ ] **B** He is lost.
- [ ] **C** He is preparing to attack Jim.
- [ ] **D** He is saying his prayers.
- [ ] **E** He is afraid of Jim.

13. What do you think has caused the strange timbre (tone) of Ben Gunn's voice?

- [ ] **A** He has been unwell.
- [ ] **B** His diet has been poor.
- [ ] **C** He is embarrassed.
- [ ] **D** He hasn't used his voice for a long time.
- [ ] **E** He has been shouting too much.

(14) A synonym for the word "fancied" (line 35) in this context is:
- [ ] **A** Liked
- [ ] **B** Plain
- [ ] **C** Unwanted
- [ ] **D** Real
- [ ] **E** Imagined

(15) What do you think Jim feels towards Ben Gunn?
- [ ] **A** Disgust
- [ ] **B** Amusement
- [ ] **C** Sympathy
- [ ] **D** Puzzlement
- [ ] **E** Anger

(16) Which of the following is the best explanation for Ben Gunn's presence on the island?
- [ ] **A** He was looking for food.
- [ ] **B** He had been abandoned there.
- [ ] **C** He was on holiday.
- [ ] **D** He had been shipwrecked.
- [ ] **E** He had always lived there.

(17) Why does Benn Gunn fall to his knees in front of Jim?
- [ ] **A** He has no energy to stand.
- [ ] **B** He is searching for oysters.
- [ ] **C** He is begging.
- [ ] **D** The sand is too hot for his feet.
- [ ] **E** He tripped over.

(18) Which two of the reasons below explain why Ben keeps touching Jim?
1. To provoke him into a fight
2. Because he likes his clothes
3. Because he is pleased to see him
4. To check that he is real
5. To check he is not injured
- [ ] **A** 4 and 3
- [ ] **B** 1 and 2
- [ ] **C** 2 and 4
- [ ] **D** 3 and 1
- [ ] **E** 5 and 2

(19) What does the phrase "you shall have cheese by the stone" mean?
- [ ] **A** You will eat cheese sitting near to a stone.
- [ ] **B** You will have a cheese as big as a stone.
- [ ] **C** You will have cheese in large quantities.
- [ ] **D** You will have very hard cheese.
- [ ] **E** You will have a cheese called Stone.

20 According to the text, Ben Gunn:

	A	Has eaten goats
	B	Hates goats
	C	Likes goats
	D	Desires goat cheese
	E	Has a pet goat

If a paragraph or sentence is confusing, re-read it and the words might make more sense.

BILLY'S AWESOME ADVERBS

Throughout *Treasure Island*, adverbs are used to describe the verbs. For example, "his eyes turned instinctively in that direction". The word "instinctively", which means automatically or with reflex, describes the turning action. Below are some sentences from *Treasure Island* with the adverbs removed. Try to find an adverb to fill in the blank. You can compare afterwards with the chosen words in the actual passage.

1)   I set my face _____ for this man of the island and walked briskly towards him.

2)   But he must have been watching me _____.

3)   _____ the figure reappeared, and making a wide circuit, began to head me off.

4)   And _____ I began to prefer the dangers that I knew to those I knew not.

5)   I turned on my heel, and looking _____ behind me over my shoulder, began to

retrace my steps in the direction of the boats.

Adverbs or adverbial phrases can come before or after a verb.

6. ANNE OF GREEN GABLES

Matthew and Marilla Cuthbert have sent for a youngster from an orphanage to help them on their farm.

1 Marilla came briskly forward as Matthew opened the door. But when her eyes fell on the odd little figure in the stiff, ugly dress, with the long braids of red hair and the eager, luminous eyes, she stopped short in amazement.

"Matthew Cuthbert, who's that?" she ejaculated. "Where is the boy?"

5 "There wasn't any boy," said Matthew wretchedly. "There was only her." He nodded at the child, remembering that he had never even asked her name.

"No boy! But there must have been a boy," insisted Marilla. "We sent word to Mrs. Spencer to bring a boy."

"Well, she didn't. She brought her. I asked the station-master. And I had to bring her
10 home. She couldn't be left there, no matter where the mistake had come in."

"Well, this is a pretty piece of business!" ejaculated Marilla.

During this dialogue the child had remained silent, her eyes roving from one to the other, all the animation fading out of her face. Suddenly she seemed to grasp the full meaning of what had been said. Dropping her precious carpet-bag she sprang forward a step and
15 clasped her hands.

"You don't want me!" she cried. "You don't want me because I'm not a boy! I might have expected it. Nobody ever did want me. I might have known it was all too beautiful to last. I might have known nobody really did want me. Oh, what shall I do? I'm going to burst into tears!"

20 Burst into tears she did. Sitting down on a chair by the table, flinging her arms out upon it, and burying her face in them, she proceeded to cry stormily. Marilla and Matthew looked at each other deprecatingly across the stove. Neither of them knew what to say or do. Finally Marilla stepped lamely into the breach.

"Well, well, there's no need to cry so about it."

25 "Yes, there is need!" The child raised her head quickly, revealing a tear-stained face and trembling lips. "You would cry, too, if you were an orphan and had come to a place you thought was going to be home and found that they didn't want you because you weren't a boy. Oh, this is the most tragical thing that ever happened to me!"

Something like a reluctant smile, rather rusty from long disuse, mellowed Marilla's grim
30 expression.

"Well, don't cry any more. We're not going to turn you out-of-doors to-night. You'll have to stay here until we investigate this affair. What's your name?"

The child hesitated for a moment.

"Will you please call me Cordelia?" she said eagerly.

35 "Call you Cordelia? Is that your name?"

"No-o-o, it's not exactly my name, but I would love to be called Cordelia. It's such a perfectly elegant name."

"I don't know what on earth you mean. If Cordelia isn't your name, what is?"

"Anne Shirley," reluctantly faltered forth the owner of that name, "but, oh, please do call
40 me Cordelia. It can't matter much to you what you call me if I'm only going to be here a little while, can it? And Anne is such an unromantic name."

"Unromantic fiddlesticks!" said the unsympathetic Marilla. "Anne is a real good plain sensible name. You've no need to be ashamed of it."

"Oh, I'm not ashamed of it," explained Anne, "only I like Cordelia better. I've always
45 imagined that my name was Cordelia—at least, I always have of late years. When I was young I used to imagine it was Geraldine, but I like Cordelia better now. But if you call me Anne please call me Anne spelled with an E."

"What difference does it make how it's spelled?" asked Marilla with another rusty smile as she picked up the teapot.

50 "Oh, it makes such a difference. It looks so much nicer. When you hear a name pronounced can't you always see it in your mind, just as if it was printed out? I can; and A-n-n looks dreadful, but A-n-n-e looks so much more distinguished. If you'll only call me Anne spelled with an E I shall try to reconcile myself to not being called Cordelia."

"Very well, then, Anne spelled with an E, can you tell us how this mistake came to be made?
55 We sent word to Mrs. Spencer to bring us a boy. Were there no boys at the asylum?"

"Oh, yes, there was an abundance of them. But Mrs. Spencer said distinctly that you wanted a girl about eleven years old. And the matron said she thought I would do. You don't know how delighted I was. I couldn't sleep all last night for joy. Oh," she added reproachfully, turning to Matthew, "why didn't you tell me at the station that you didn't
60 want me and leave me there? If I hadn't seen the White Way of Delight and the Lake of Shining Waters it wouldn't be so hard."

"What on earth does she mean?" demanded Marilla, staring at Matthew.

"She—she's just referring to some conversation we had on the road," said Matthew hastily. "I'm going out to put the mare in, Marilla. Have tea ready when I come back."

6. ANNE OF GREEN GABLES questions

1. Why does the text say Marilla "stopped short in amazement" when she saw the child?
   - [ ] **A** The child looked peculiar.
   - [ ] **B** The child was staring back at her.
   - [ ] **C** Matthew opened the door too quickly.
   - [ ] **D** Marilla was expecting to see a boy.
   - [ ] **E** Matthew had forgotten to ask the child's name.

2. Which of the following statements is not true about the child?
   - [ ] **A** The child is a girl.
   - [ ] **B** The child seems ugly.
   - [ ] **C** The child is a red-head.
   - [ ] **D** The child's hair is plaited.
   - [ ] **E** The child is small.

3. What is the best synonym for the word "luminous" as used in the text? (line 3)
   - [ ] **A** Large
   - [ ] **B** Glow-in-the-dark
   - [ ] **C** Bright
   - [ ] **D** Dark
   - [ ] **E** Lurid

4. Why did Matthew bring the child home with him?
   - [ ] **A** He thought she would be useful.
   - [ ] **B** The station-master told him to.
   - [ ] **C** Matthew liked the child.
   - [ ] **D** He knew there had been a mistake.
   - [ ] **E** Matthew didn't want to leave her alone at the station.

5. Which part of speech is the word "animation"?
   - [ ] **A** A verb
   - [ ] **B** An adjective
   - [ ] **C** An adverb
   - [ ] **D** A preposition
   - [ ] **E** A noun

6. In lines 14 and 15, Anne drops "her precious carpet-bag, she sprang forward a step and clasped her hands".
   What is the best explanation for why she acted in this way?
   - [ ] **A** She realised that Matthew and Marilla wanted a boy, not her.
   - [ ] **B** Her bag was too heavy to carry any further.
   - [ ] **C** She was angry about what had been said.
   - [ ] **D** She wanted to stretch her legs.
   - [ ] **E** She wanted to plead with Matthew and Marilla to let her stay.

⑦   What is the best definition of the adverb "deprecatingly"? (line 22)

     ☐   **A**   Unappreciatively

     ☐   **B**   Disapprovingly

     ☐   **C**   Uncertainly

     ☐   **D**   Unhappily

     ☐   **E**   Depressingly

⑧   Why was the child crying?

     ☐   **A**   Because she was an orphan

     ☐   **B**   Because she thought her life was tragic

     ☐   **C**   Because she understood that she was not wanted

     ☐   **D**   Because she had no home

     ☐   **E**   None of the above

⑨   What does the description of Marilla's expression tell you about her? (line 29)

     ☐   **A**   She hasn't smiled much for a long time.

     ☐   **B**   She is an unhappy person.

     ☐   **C**   She is a serious and forbidding person.

     ☐   **D**   She is an unkind, hostile person.

     ☐   **E**   She does not like the look of the child.

⑩   How does Marilla try to stop the child from crying?

     ☐   **A**   She promises to find out what has gone wrong.

     ☐   **B**   She asks her name.

     ☐   **C**   She promises to keep the child.

     ☐   **D**   She confirms that they will let her stay that night.

     ☐   **E**   She gives her a warm drink.

⑪   What is the child's first name?

     ☐   **A**   Cordelia

     ☐   **B**   Shirley

     ☐   **C**   Anne

     ☐   **D**   Geraldine

     ☐   **E**   Marilla

⑫   Why does the child ask to be called Cordelia?

     ☐   **A**   It is her name

     ☐   **B**   She does not know how to spell her real name

     ☐   **C**   She thinks Anne is a sensible name

     ☐   **D**   The child considers Cordelia to be a graceful, stylish name

     ☐   **E**   The child's second name is Cordelia

13. What does the discussion about names tell us about the characters of Anne and Marilla?
1. Marilla is unsympathetic.
3. Marilla is down-to-earth.
2. Anne enjoys make-believe.
4. Anne is dishonest.

- A   1 and 2
- B   2 and 4
- C   1 and 4
- D   2 and 3
- E   3 and 4

14. What is the best definition of the word "fiddlesticks" as used in this text? (line 42)
- A   An eager exclamation
- B   An exclamation meaning "stuff and nonsense"
- C   A cry of delight.
- D   The bow of a violin
- E   A magical, mystical word similar to "abracadabra"

15. What are "late years" as used by Anne? (line 45)
- A   Years to come later
- B   Years that were a long time ago
- C   Years that Anne can remember well
- D   Years that Anne is imagining
- E   Years that have recently passed

16. What reasons does Anne give to explain why she wants her name to be spelt with an 'E'?
- A   "Ann" is pronounced differently.
- B   Marilla prefers Ann.
- C   She prefers longer names.
- D   She feels "Anne" looks more distinctive and worthy of respect.
- E   She has never been sure how her name was intended to be spelt.

17. What is the best definition of the word "abundance"? (line 56)
- A   A very large quantity
- B   Overflowing
- C   Very few indeed
- D   Hard to distinguish
- E   Abandoned

18. Where are "The White Way of Delight" and "The Lake of Shining Waters"?
- A   In Anne's imagination
- B   Places in a book Anne has been reading
- C   Things she has seen on her journey from the station
- D   Places she knew from the asylum
- E   None of the above

(19) How is this text written?

- ☐ **A** First person narrative
- ☐ **B** First person report
- ☐ **C** Third person narrative
- ☐ **D** First person diary
- ☐ **E** Third person recount

(20) What do you think will happen next in the book?

1. Anne will be sent back to the asylum.
2. Anne will be allowed to stay with Matthew and Marilla.
3. Matthew and Marilla will find Anne troublesome but endearing.
4. Matthew and Marilla will regret the decision they make.

- ☐ **A** 1 and 3
- ☐ **B** 2 and 3
- ☐ **C** 1 and 4
- ☐ **D** 2 and 4
- ☐ **E** 3 and 4

If you come across an unfamiliar word, try to use the surrounding words to help establish the meaning.

BILLY'S RIGOROUS REPORTING CLAUSES

Reporting clauses indicate who is talking or thinking. They can also add more detail, for example, they can tell us *how* someone said something. Throughout *Anne of Green Gables* they are used to emphasise emotion. How many can you spot in the passage? Try to place the correct reporting clause at the end of the following lines of speech.

1) "Matthew Cuthbert, who's that?" _____

2) "You don't want me!" _____

3) "Will you please call me Cordelia?" _____

4) "Oh, I'm not ashamed of it," _____

5) "Unromantic fiddlesticks!" _____

6) "What difference does it make how it's spelled?" _____

explained Anne

she ejaculated

asked Marilla

she cried

said the unsympathetic Marilla

she said eagerly

Using different words to "said" can help describe how words are spoken. Often, descriptive reporting clauses can add more emotion to a text.

7. OLIVER TWIST

Oliver has been apprenticed to an undertaker. Noah Claypole and the undertaker's other apprentices are jealous of Oliver's popularity with their employer.

1 And now, I come to a very important passage in Oliver's history; for I have to record an act, slight and unimportant perhaps in appearance, but which indirectly produced a material change in all his future prospects and proceedings.

One day, Oliver and Noah had descended into the kitchen at the usual dinner-hour, to
5 banquet upon a small joint of mutton—a pound and a half of the worst end of the neck— when Charlotte being called out of the way, there ensued a brief interval of time, which Noah Claypole, being hungry and vicious, considered he could not possibly devote to a worthier purpose than aggravating and tantalising young Oliver Twist.

Intent upon this innocent amusement, Noah put his feet on the table-cloth; and pulled
10 Oliver's hair; and twitched his ears; and expressed his opinion that he was a 'sneak'; and furthermore announced his intention of coming to see him hanged, whenever that desirable event should take place; and entered upon various topics of petty annoyance, like a malicious and ill-conditioned charity-boy as he was. But, none of these taunts producing the desired effect of making Oliver cry, Noah attempted to be more facetious
15 still; and in his attempt, did what many small wits, with far greater reputations than Noah, sometimes do to this day, when they want to be funny. He got rather personal.

"Work'us," said Noah, "how's your mother?"

"She's dead," replied Oliver; "don't you say anything about her to me!"

Oliver's colour rose as he said this; he breathed quickly; and there was a curious working
20 of the mouth and nostrils, which Mr. Claypole thought must be the immediate precursor of a violent fit of crying. Under this impression he returned to the charge.

"What did she die of, Work'us?" said Noah.

"Of a broken heart, some of our old nurses told me," replied Oliver: more as if he were talking to himself, than answering Noah. "I think I know what it must be to die of that!"

25 "Tol de rol lol lol, right fol lairy, Work'us," said Noah, as a tear rolled down Oliver's cheek.

"What's set you a snivelling now?"

"Not YOU," replied Oliver, hastily brushing the tear away. "Don't think about it."

"Oh , not me, eh!" sneered Noah.

"No, not you," replied Oliver sharply. "There; that's enough. Don't say anything more to
30 me about her; you'd better not!"

"Better not!" exclaimed Noah. "Well! Better not! Work'us, don't be impudent. YOUR mother, too!"

"She was a nice 'un she was. Oh, Lor!" And here, Noah nodded his head expressively; and curled up as much of his small red nose as muscular action could collect together, for
35 the occasion.

"Yer know, Work'us," continued Noah, emboldened by Oliver's silence, and speaking in a jeering tone of affected pity: of all tones the most annoying: "Yer know, Work'us, it can't be helped now; and of course yer couldn't help it then; and I am very sorry for it; and I'm sure we all are, and pity yer very much. But yer must know, Work'us, yer mother was a
40 regular right-down bad 'un."

"What did you say?" inquired Oliver, looking up very quickly.

"A regular right-down bad 'un, Work'us," replied Noah, coolly. "And it's a great deal better, Work'us, that she died when she did, or else she'd have been hard labouring in Bridewell, or transported, or hung; which is more likely than either, isn't it?"

45 Crimson with fury, Oliver started up; overthrew the chair and table; seized Noah by the throat; shook him, in the violence of his rage, till his teeth chattered in his head; and collecting his whole force into one heavy blow, felled him to the ground.

A minute ago, the boy had looked the quiet child, mild, dejected creature that harsh treatment had made him. But his spirit was roused at last; the cruel insult to his dead mother
50 had set his blood on fire. His breast heaved; his attitude was erect; his eye bright and vivid; his whole person changed, as he stood glaring over the cowardly tormentor who now lay crouching at his feet; and defied him with an energy he had never known before.

"He'll murder me!" blubbered Noah. "Charlotte! Missis! Here's the new boy a murdering of me! Help! help! Oliver's gone mad! Char--lotte!"

55 Noah's shouts were responded to, by a loud scream from Charlotte, and a louder from Mrs. Sowerberry; the former of whom rushed into the kitchen by a side-door, while the latter paused on the staircase till she was quite certain that it was consistent with the preservation of human life, to come further down.

7. OLIVER TWIST questions

1. Which is the best synonym for the word "taunts"? (line 13)
   - [ ] **A** Jeers
   - [ ] **B** Jives
   - [ ] **C** Compliments
   - [ ] **D** Tricks
   - [ ] **E** Sympathises

2. Why does Noah continue to ask Oliver about his mother after Oliver has asked him not to?
   - [ ] **A** He wants to find out about her.
   - [ ] **B** He wants to upset Oliver.
   - [ ] **C** He has no mother of his own.
   - [ ] **D** He feels sorry for Oliver.
   - [ ] **E** He doesn't believe that Oliver has one.

3. What makes Oliver say "I think I know what it must be to die of that"? (line 24)
   - [ ] **A** Oliver believes that he has his mother's heart.
   - [ ] **B** Oliver has read about death in a book.
   - [ ] **C** Oliver feels that his heart is broken.
   - [ ] **D** Oliver wants to break Noah's heart.
   - [ ] **E** He is worried that he has a medical problem with his heart.

4. This event in Oliver's life is important because:
   - [ ] **A** It upsets him.
   - [ ] **B** He never forgets it.
   - [ ] **C** He sustains an injury.
   - [ ] **D** It changes the course of his life.
   - [ ] **E** He meets someone important.

5. Why does Oliver hastily brush the tear away from his cheek?
   - [ ] **A** He does not want to appear upset.
   - [ ] **B** He has no handkerchief.
   - [ ] **C** He wants to stop it stinging his face.
   - [ ] **D** It is an involuntary action.
   - [ ] **E** He does not want to make Noah feel bad.

6. The word "immediate" (line 20) is:
   - [ ] **A** An adjective
   - [ ] **B** A noun
   - [ ] **C** An adverb
   - [ ] **D** A pronoun
   - [ ] **E** A preposition

7. Which of these words best describes the character of Noah?

   ☐ **A**   Witty
   ☐ **B**   Obnoxious
   ☐ **C**   Inquisitive
   ☐ **D**   Gracious
   ☐ **E**   Sympathetic

8. Why doesn't Mrs Sowerberry enter the kitchen immediately?

   ☐ **A**   The door is stuck.
   ☐ **B**   She is too fat to get through the door.
   ☐ **C**   Charlotte screams to warn her not to go.
   ☐ **D**   She left something upstairs.
   ☐ **E**   She is frightened that someone might be murdered.

9. Which of the following two statements describe Noah's reaction to Oliver's attack?

1. He cries.
2. He fights back.
3. He calls Mrs Sowerberry and Charlotte for help.
4. He calls Charlotte for help.
5. He runs away.

   ☐ **A**   2 and 3
   ☐ **B**   2 and 4
   ☐ **C**   1 and 4
   ☐ **D**   1 and 3
   ☐ **E**   1 and 5

10. Why does Noah remain unafraid of Oliver despite Oliver's warning that he had better not say anything more?

   ☐ **A**   He is bigger than Oliver.
   ☐ **B**   There is no-one else there.
   ☐ **C**   Oliver apologises.
   ☐ **D**   He is too stupid to understand the threat.
   ☐ **E**   He thinks that Oliver is a wimp.

11. If Oliver's mother had not died, Noah asserts that she would most likely have been:

   ☐ **A**   Sentenced to death
   ☐ **B**   Sent to Australia
   ☐ **C**   Working in Bridewell
   ☐ **D**   Living with Oliver
   ☐ **E**   Rich and happy

12. Oliver was inclined to violent behaviour:

   ☐ **A**   Often
   ☐ **B**   Rarely
   ☐ **C**   On Saturdays and Sundays
   ☐ **D**   Never
   ☐ **E**   When he was hungry

13. What might be the reason for Oliver's lack of aggression?

- [ ] **A**   He was born with a passive character.
- [ ] **B**   He has been bullied in the past.
- [ ] **C**   His mother told him not to fight.
- [ ] **D**   He is not very strong.
- [ ] **E**   He thinks fighting is wrong.

14. Before the incidents in the text, Oliver was:

- [ ] **A**   In the kitchen
- [ ] **B**   Working at the undertaker's premises
- [ ] **C**   Upstairs
- [ ] **D**   Outside playing
- [ ] **E**   At the next-door neighbour's

15. When the narrator says that Noah is indulging in "innocent amusement" (line 9), he means that Noah:

- [ ] **A**   Is not guilty of doing anything wrong
- [ ] **B**   Is too naïve to understand the consequences of his actions
- [ ] **C**   Looking forward to a smoothie for tea
- [ ] **D**   Does not know that he is being mean
- [ ] **E**   Is not doing anything illegal

16. Which of these words is a synonym for "snivelling" (line 26)?

- [ ] **A**   Bawling
- [ ] **B**   Spinning
- [ ] **C**   Sobbing
- [ ] **D**   Sneering
- [ ] **E**   Upset

17. Noah says of Oliver's mother "she was a nice'un she was. Oh, Lor!" This is an example of:

- [ ] **A**   Sarcasm
- [ ] **B**   Alliteration
- [ ] **C**   Irony
- [ ] **D**   Imagery
- [ ] **E**   A metaphor

18. Which word best describes the expression of Noah's face? (lines 33 and 34)

- [ ] **A**   Grimacing
- [ ] **B**   Smiling
- [ ] **C**   Amazement
- [ ] **D**   Sneering
- [ ] **E**   Sorrow

19. When Oliver finally loses self-control, firstly he:

- [ ] **A**   Calls for help
- [ ] **B**   Punches Noah to the ground
- [ ] **C**   Kicks Noah
- [ ] **D**   Breaks a window
- [ ] **E**   Turns the table over

20 In your opinion, what is Oliver implying when he warns Noah "you'd better not"?

	A	That Noah might break something
	B	That Noah is losing his temper
	C	That Oliver is finding it funny
	D	That someone might overhear
	E	That Oliver is losing his temper

After marking your work, a really useful activity is to highlight where in the text you found the answer. This will hone your detective skills.

BILLY'S CLEVER COMMAS

Commas can be used to shorten lengthy sentences or clauses. In *Oliver Twist*, semicolons are often inserted. Like commas, semi-colons can indicate a pause – slightly longer than the pause indicated by a comma but shorter than the pause indicated by a full-stop.

In the passage below, try to place the 15 omitted commas and semi-colons.

> Intent upon this innocent amusement Noah put his feet on the table-cloth and pulled Oliver's hair and twitched his ears and expressed his opinion that he was a 'sneak' and furthermore announced his intention of coming to see him hanged whenever that desirable event should take place and entered upon various topics of petty annoyance like a malicious and ill-conditioned charity-boy as he was. But none of these taunts producing the desired effect of making Oliver cry Noah attempted to be more facetious still and in his attempt did what many small wits with far greater reputations than Noah sometimes do to this day when they want to be funny. He got rather personal.

You can check in the answers to see if you found all the commas and semi-colons.

Commas can be used to separate items in a list. They also mark out the subordinate clause in a sentence.

8. COMING TO AMERICA

1 **Earliest Visitors**

"In fourteen hundred and ninety-two Columbus sailed the ocean blue."

This rhyme was chanted by schoolchildren for many years to learn when America was "discovered" by Christopher Columbus. But was he really the first person to arrive in this
5 land?

We all know nowadays that he was not. Long before 1492, in what historians now call the Pre-Columbian Era, native Americans lived on the continent of North America, now USA and Canada. If you had been one of these people, you might have hunted game – bison and deer; you may have fished for salmon and would probably have had a nomadic
10 life, following the animals over great plains.

We also now believe that Vikings were the first settlers to come to America from Europe. Archaeologists have found the remains of a settlement in Newfoundland which dates from the year AD1000, almost 500 years before Christopher Columbus made his famous voyage.

15 **A Route West to India**

When Christopher Columbus stood on the deck of his ship the "Santa Maria" watching the sun setting in the west, he was seeking a new trade route to the East Indies (what we now call Asia). Most people by then believed a new idea: that the world was round, not flat, and Christopher was convinced that sailing in a westerly direction would lead him
20 round the world to familiar trading lands. You can imagine his excitement when first he spotted the green trees and hills of undiscovered islands for the first time. Columbus and his crew knew nothing of America – they believed that the lands they saw were part of India and so they named these islands the West Indies – a name that remains to this day.

Voyages of Pilgrims

25 On 6th September 1620 a small ship called "The Mayflower" set sail from Plymouth Harbour on a journey across the Atlantic to what was now known as The New World. On board were about one hundred and thirty puritans seeking religious freedom to live and worship God the way they wanted to. These travellers are known today as 'Pilgrim Fathers'. Others followed and by 1635 there were enough skilled farmers, tradesmen,
30 craftsmen and intellectuals to found their own university – Harvard, which is today one of the most prestigious in the world.

It is also these settlers who celebrated the first "Thanksgiving" – America's famous holiday. It is told that after the first harvest, the pilgrims celebrated and gave thanks to God, alongside 90 native Americans who had advised them on farming the land.

An Evil Trade

Not everyone who made the hazardous journey across the Atlantic did so in the hope of a better life. Many Americans today can trace their ancestry back to Africans brought over in chains as slaves to work on sugar and cotton plantations and sold in exchange for goods such as guns and brandy. This cruel trade and slavery itself was finally outlawed in 1865 after the American Civil War. Now we recognise it as a shameful crime against humanity.

The Land of Opportunity

Most people nowadays know the famous Statue of Liberty which stands in New York Harbour. Her presence, with arm outstretched, was of great significance to the many immigrants of the 19th and 20th century who made the journey from Europe, escaping crop failures, unemployment, religious persecution and famine in search of a better life in America, the "land of opportunity". Liberty stands next to Ellis Island, the gateway to the United States. After an arduous sea journey, many passengers described their first glimpse of the statue and how they disembarked and queued with their possessions on Ellis Island for medical and legal inspections before being allowed onto American soil.

LHR – JFK

Even today many people seek a new life, living and working in America. For these hopefuls there are no long sea voyages or medical examinations. Instead, having acquired a visa from the US Embassy, they fly across the Atlantic in a few hours from places such as London's Heathrow Airport to New York's John F Kennedy Airport. Just like their predecessors, they find themselves stepping out under the sun shining upon them in another land, a "New World" and know that they too are coming to America.

8. COMING TO AMERICA questions

1. According to this text, when did Christopher Columbus first sail to America?
   - [ ] **A** Many years ago
   - [ ] **B** 1400
   - [ ] **C** 1492
   - [ ] **D** Before 1492
   - [ ] **E** AD 1000

2. Which of the following statements about Native Americans is not described in the text?
   - [ ] **A** They hunted bison and deer.
   - [ ] **B** They travelled over the plains.
   - [ ] **C** They were fishermen.
   - [ ] **D** They lived in tepees.
   - [ ] **E** They were nomads.

3. Why do archaeologists believe that the Vikings sailed as far as America?
   - [ ] **A** They found the remains of a Viking settlement.
   - [ ] **B** They discovered a Viking ship.
   - [ ] **C** Archaeologists knew they were there 500 years before Columbus.
   - [ ] **D** Columbus met some Vikings.
   - [ ] **E** None of the above

4. What is the meaning of the word "chanted"? (line 3)
   - [ ] **A** Sang together
   - [ ] **B** Learnt by heart
   - [ ] **C** Repeated in a sing-song tone
   - [ ] **D** Forgot the words of
   - [ ] **E** Thought

5. Why did Christopher Columbus make his first voyage?
   - [ ] **A** He wanted to sail around the world.
   - [ ] **B** He wanted to discover America.
   - [ ] **C** He wanted to leave Europe.
   - [ ] **D** He wanted to find a trade route to Asia.
   - [ ] **E** He wanted to see Native Americans.

6. Which direction was he travelling?
   - [ ] **A** North
   - [ ] **B** West
   - [ ] **C** South
   - [ ] **D** East
   - [ ] **E** Towards the equator

7. What part of speech is the word "familiar"? (line 20)
- [ ] **A** A noun
- [ ] **B** A verb
- [ ] **C** An adjective
- [ ] **D** An adverb
- [ ] **E** A preposition

8. Why did the islands Columbus sailed to become known as the West Indies according to the text?
- [ ] **A** They were west of India.
- [ ] **B** Columbus knew nothing of America.
- [ ] **C** The Native Americans had named them already.
- [ ] **D** Columbus thought he had sailed as far as India.
- [ ] **E** The islands looked like familiar trading lands.

9. What was the name of the ship which sailed from Plymouth in 1620?
- [ ] **A** The Santa Maria
- [ ] **B** The Mayflower
- [ ] **C** The Puritan
- [ ] **D** Columbia
- [ ] **E** None of the above

10. Why did the Pilgrim Fathers sail to America in 1620?
- [ ] **A** They sought freedom to worship God in the way they wanted.
- [ ] **B** They wanted to farm a new land.
- [ ] **C** They were looking for adventure.
- [ ] **D** They aimed to develop their crafts.
- [ ] **E** They relocated to follow in the footsteps of Christopher Columbus.

11. Which option is the closest in meaning to the word "prestigious"? (line 31)
- [ ] **A** Famous
- [ ] **B** High status
- [ ] **C** Upmarket
- [ ] **D** Intelligent
- [ ] **E** Expensive

12. What was the first "Thanksgiving"?
- [ ] **A** A prayer
- [ ] **B** A lesson in farming from Native Americans
- [ ] **C** A harvest festival
- [ ] **D** A holiday
- [ ] **E** A day where no one worked

13. What is the best antonym for the word "hazardous"? (line 36)
- [ ] **A** Dangerous
- [ ] **B** Perilous
- [ ] **C** Conventional
- [ ] **D** Cautious
- [ ] **E** Safe

⑭ Where does the Statue of Liberty stand today?
- [ ] **A** On Ellis Island
- [ ] **B** In New York Harbour (or Harbor)
- [ ] **C** At Harvard University
- [ ] **D** In a museum
- [ ] **E** Away from American soil

⑮ Which of the following is not mentioned in the text as a reason for 19th and 20th century migrants wanting to go to America?
- [ ] **A** To escape crop failures
- [ ] **B** To avoid unemployment
- [ ] **C** To escape from starvation
- [ ] **D** To improve their education
- [ ] **E** To avoid persecution for religious beliefs

⑯ In the text what are LHR and JFK?
- [ ] **A** Bridges
- [ ] **B** Embassys
- [ ] **C** Airports
- [ ] **D** Aeroplanes
- [ ] **E** Examinations

⑰ Which of the following terms are used to refer to America in the text?
1. Ellis Island
2. The New World
3. The Undiscovered Land
4. The Land of Opportunity
- [ ] **A** 1 and 2
- [ ] **B** 1 and 3
- [ ] **C** 2 and 3
- [ ] **D** 2 and 4
- [ ] **E** 3 and 4

⑱ What is the Pre-Columbian Era?
- [ ] **A** The time before the Statue of Liberty was built
- [ ] **B** The time before the Vikings arrived
- [ ] **C** The time when Native Americans roamed the plains
- [ ] **D** The time before people lived in America
- [ ] **E** The time up until 1492

⑲ Which of the following are not mentioned in the text?
- [ ] **A** Explorers
- [ ] **B** Slaves
- [ ] **C** Pilgrims
- [ ] **D** Migrants
- [ ] **E** Holidaymakers

20 What type of text do you consider this to be?

- [ ] **A** Diary
- [ ] **B** Historical novel
- [ ] **C** Story
- [ ] **D** Informative text
- [ ] **E** Poem

Underlining a keyword or an important phrase will help you retain that piece of information. Don't underline whole texts – this will waste time!

BILLY'S EXCITING EMOTIONS

'Coming to America' is a step back in time and describes the earliest visitors to America. Here we would like you to imagine you are Christopher Columbus and write an emotive paragraph to describe when he first spotted the green trees and hills of the undiscovered islands of the West Indies. A list of emotive words which should be included is given below.

overwhelmed	overjoyed	elated	euphoric	exuberant	suspicious
sceptical	privileged	satisfied	thrilled	exhausted	astonished

_____

_____

_____

_____

_____

_____

_____

_____

_____

_____

Did you use all the words above in your descriptive paragraph?

Questions in comprehensions often relate to how a character feels. Remember to think about the character's emotions as you are reading the passage or extract.

9. YOU ARE OLD, FATHER WILLIAM

15:00
15 minutes

1   "You are old, Father William," the young man said,
    "And your hair has become very white;
    And yet you incessantly stand on your head –
    Do you think, at your age, it is right?"

5   "In my youth," Father William replied to his son,
    "I feared it might injure the brain;
    But, now that I'm perfectly sure I have none,
    Why, I do it again and again."

    "You are old," said the youth, "as I mentioned before,
10 And have grown most uncommonly fat;
    Yet you turned a back-somersault in at the door –
    Pray, what is the reason of that?"

    "In my youth," said the sage, as he shook his grey locks,
    "I kept all my limbs very supple
15 By the use of this ointment – one shilling the box –
    Allow me to sell you a couple?"

    "You are old," said the youth, "and your jaws are too weak
    For anything tougher than suet;
    Yet you finished the goose, with the bones and the beak –
20 Pray, how did you manage to do it?"

    "In my youth," said his father, "I took to the law,
    And argued each case with my wife;
    And the muscular strength, which it gave to my jaw,
    Has lasted the rest of my life."

25 "You are old," said the youth, "one would hardly suppose
    That your eye was as steady as ever;
    Yet you balanced an eel on the end of your nose –
    What made you so awfully clever?"

    "I have answered three questions, and that is enough,"
30 Said his father; "don't give yourself airs!
    Do you think I can listen all day to such stuff?
    Be off, or I'll kick you downstairs!"

Lewis Carroll (1865)

9. YOU ARE OLD, FATHER WILLIAM questions

① Which two strange things does Father William do?
1.   Stands on his head
2.   Injures his brain
3.   Turns somersaults
4.   Eats the bones and feet of a duck
5.   Falls down the stairs

- ☐ **A**   1 and 2
- ☐ **B**   1 and 3
- ☐ **C**   2 and 5
- ☐ **D**   3 and 4
- ☐ **E**   1 and 5

② Why does the boy think that Father William should not be able to do a somersault?
- ☐ **A**   He is old and weak.
- ☐ **B**   He is old and skinny and walks with a stick.
- ☐ **C**   He is old and corpulent.
- ☐ **D**   He is too old to remember how to do it.
- ☐ **E**   He has not had lessons.

③ Why did Father William change his mind about the wisdom of standing on his head?
- ☐ **A**   He injured his brain.
- ☐ **B**   He had no proof that it harmed him.
- ☐ **C**   He was frightened of breaking his limbs.
- ☐ **D**   He really enjoyed doing it.
- ☐ **E**   He decided he had no brain.

④ Why is the boy surprised that Father William could balance an eel on his nose?
- ☐ **A**   Eels are slippery.
- ☐ **B**   He didn't think that Father William would be able to see very well.
- ☐ **C**   He thought Father William wasn't agile enough.
- ☐ **D**   Fish smell nasty.
- ☐ **E**   Father William has a small nose

⑤ Why does Father William offer to sell the boy some ointment?
- ☐ **A**   Because the boy has hurt his finger.
- ☐ **B**   Because Father William is poor and needs to make money.
- ☐ **C**   So that the boy can stay supple.
- ☐ **D**   So that the boy might be able to turn somersaults too.
- ☐ **E**   Because it is cheap.

6. The man has acquired strong jaws by:
   - [ ] **A**   Obeying the law
   - [ ] **B**   Shouting at his wife
   - [ ] **C**   Carrying a suitcase in his teeth
   - [ ] **D**   Talking a lot about matters of the law with his wife
   - [ ] **E**   Chewing a lot of suet

7. The youth is surprised that Father William:
   - [ ] **A**   Is unable to eat suet
   - [ ] **B**   Eats only suet
   - [ ] **C**   Is able to eat the bones and beak of a goose
   - [ ] **D**   Is so greedy
   - [ ] **E**   Does not remember his manners when eating

8. The youth asks four questions. Why does Father William only answer three?
   - [ ] **A**   He can't hear him very well.
   - [ ] **B**   He doesn't know the answer to the third.
   - [ ] **C**   He wants to kick him down the stairs.
   - [ ] **D**   He has got something else to do.
   - [ ] **E**   He is losing his patience.

9. The youth says to Father William: "Do you think at your age it is right?" Do you think he is being:
   - [ ] **A**   Concerned and anxious?
   - [ ] **B**   Clever and funny?
   - [ ] **C**   Amusing and entertaining?
   - [ ] **D**   Critical and insensitive?
   - [ ] **E**   Stupid?

10. Which of these words best describes the youth?
    - [ ] **A**   Courteous
    - [ ] **B**   Tactful
    - [ ] **C**   Inquisitive
    - [ ] **D**   Meddlesome
    - [ ] **E**   Kind

11. Which word below is a synonym for "incessantly" (line 3)?
    - [ ] **A**   Cleverly
    - [ ] **B**   Constantly
    - [ ] **C**   Eagerly
    - [ ] **D**   Precariously
    - [ ] **E**   Occasionally

12 To "give yourself airs" means to:
   A   Pretend to be better than you are
   B   Be proud of yourself
   C   Give yourself some praise
   D   Give yourself a present
   E   Pretend to be a ghost

13 In the context of line 14, what does the word "supple" mean?
   A   Strong
   B   Flexible
   C   Fast
   D   Obscure
   E   Smooth

14 What makes Father William a "sage"?
   A   He is slow to answer questions.
   B   He is wise enough to answer the questions.
   C   He can do a somersault.
   D   He has white hair.
   E   He is old.

15 Was Father William always overweight?
   A   No, he has grown fat later in life.
   B   No, he is slender.
   C   Yes, he has always been obese.
   D   We are not told.
   E   He has always been lean.

16 The word "perfectly" is which part of speech? (line 7)
   A   An adjective
   B   An adverb
   C   A preposition
   D   A pronoun
   E   A noun

17 The word "pray" in line 20 asks Father William to:
   A   Please tell me
   B   Say a prayer
   C   Think about
   D   Hunt for an excuse
   E   Kneel down

18 If the boy purchased a couple of boxes of the ointment offered, how much would he pay?
   A   One shilling
   B   Nothing
   C   Two shillings
   D   Five pounds
   E   Three shillings

19. Why did Father William "argue" with his wife?

- **A** Because he is bad tempered
- **B** Because she is ignorant
- **C** To exercise his jaw
- **D** Because she breaks his suitcase
- **E** To practise his legal skills

20. How did the old man enter the room?

- **A** Walking backwards
- **B** Turning a back-somersault
- **C** Doing a handstand
- **D** In a wheelchair
- **E** On his tiptoes

When answering the multiple choice questions, first eliminate the wrong answers to help limit your options.

BILLY'S SPECIAL SPEECH MARKS

In the 'You are Old, Father William', there are speech marks in every verse. Can you insert the missing speech marks in verse 1?

> You are old, Father William, the young man said,
> And your hair has become very white;
> And yet you incessantly stand on your head -
> Do you think, at your age, it is right?

Other punctuation marks are also used in this poem and it is important to recognise these as you read to help with expression and meaning.

Can you match the name of the punctuation mark to the correct symbol? Write the symbols in the empty column in the table below.

Name of the punctuation mark	Symbol
semi-colon	
hyphen	
exclamation mark	
question mark	
comma	
apostrophe	
colon	

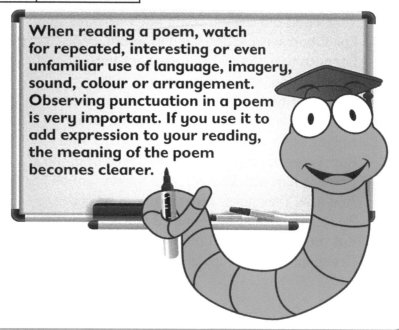

When reading a poem, watch for repeated, interesting or even unfamiliar use of language, imagery, sound, colour or arrangement. Observing punctuation in a poem is very important. If you use it to add expression to your reading, the meaning of the poem becomes clearer.

10. A MIDSUMMER NIGHT'S DREAM

ACT II., SCENE I

Oberon and Titania, King and Queen of the fairies, have had an argument. In this passage two of their servants, Puck and a Fairy, meet and have a conversation.

A wood near Athens
Enter a FAIRY at one door, and PUCK at another

1   *Puck:* How now, spirit! Whither wander thee?
    Fairy: Over hill, over dale,
    Thorough bush, thorough brier,
    Over park, over pale,
5   Thorough flood, thorough fire,
    I do wander every where,
    Swifter than the moon's sphere;
    And I serve the Fairy Queen,
    To dew her orbs upon the green.
10 The cowslips tall her pensioners be;
    In their gold coats spots you see;
    Those be rubies, fairy favours,
    In those freckles live their savours.

    I must go seek some dewdrops here,
15 And hang a pearl in every cowslip's ear.
    Farewell, thou lob of spirits; I'll be gone.
    Our Queen and all her elves come here anon.
    Puck: The King doth keep his revels here tonight;
    Take heed the Queen come not within his sight;
20 For Oberon is passing fell and wrath,
    Because that she as her attendant hath
    A lovely boy, stolen from an Indian king.
    She never had so sweet a changeling;
    And jealous Oberon would have the child
25 Knight of his train, to trace the forests wild;
    But she perforce withholds the loved boy,
    Crowns him with flowers, and makes him all her joy.
    And now they never meet in grove or green,
    By fountain clear, or spangled starlight sheen,
30 But they do square, that all their elves for fear
    Creep into acorn cups and hide them there.

10. A MIDSUMMER NIGHT'S DREAM questions

1. What question does Puck ask the Fairy (line 1)?
   - ☐ **A** Where are you going?
   - ☐ **B** How are you?
   - ☐ **C** Why are you wandering?
   - ☐ **D** When will you come back?
   - ☐ **E** Where is the Fairy Queen?

2. Where does the fairy wander?
   1. Over hills and valleys
   2. Thorough water and forests
   3. Thorough water and fires
   4. Over hills to the moon
   - ☐ **A** 1 and 2
   - ☐ **B** 1 and 3
   - ☐ **C** 2 and 3
   - ☐ **D** 2 and 4
   - ☐ **E** All of the above

3. "Swifter than the moon's sphere"
   How does this describe the fairy's flight?
   - ☐ **A** The moon's sphere is quicker than her.
   - ☐ **B** She flies around the moon and back.
   - ☐ **C** She flies in a circle like the moon.
   - ☐ **D** The moon rotates as she flies.
   - ☐ **E** She flies more quickly than the moon.

4. Look at the first four lines of the fairy's speech. Which literacy features are used here?
   "Over hill, over dale,
   Thorough bush, thorough brier,
   Over park, over pale,
   Thorough flood, thorough fire"
   1. Deliberate repetition
   2. Rhyme
   3. Alliteration
   4. Onomatopoeia
   5. A simile
   - ☐ **A** 1, 3, 5
   - ☐ **B** 2, 3, 5
   - ☐ **C** 1, 2, 3
   - ☐ **D** 3, 4, 5
   - ☐ **E** 2, 3, 4

5 "And I serve the Fairy Queen,
To dew her orbs upon the green."
What is the best explanation of what the fairy does to serve Titania, her Queen?

- [ ] **A** Dances for her on the grass
- [ ] **B** Cleans the green grass with dew
- [ ] **C** Sends the rain onto the grass
- [ ] **D** Sprinkles drops of water onto her fairy rings
- [ ] **E** Polishes her jewellery with dew

6 Who, or what, according to the fairy, would you find wearing spotted gold coats?

- [ ] **A** Elderly gentlemen
- [ ] **B** The cattle on the green
- [ ] **C** Other fairies
- [ ] **D** Meadow flowers
- [ ] **E** Titania, Queen of the Fairies

7 What is the best antonym for the word "seek"? (line 14)

- [ ] **A** Find
- [ ] **B** Discover
- [ ] **C** Hide
- [ ] **D** See
- [ ] **E** Hoard

8 The fairy tells Puck that she must "hang a pearl in every cowslip's ear" (line 14). How is the word "pearl" used here?

- [ ] **A** As a verb
- [ ] **B** As a metaphor
- [ ] **C** As an adjective
- [ ] **D** As a simile
- [ ] **E** As a pronoun

9 What does the fairy say is going to happen after she has gone?

- [ ] **A** She doesn't know who is coming to the wood.
- [ ] **B** The Queen is bringing some unknown elves to the wood.
- [ ] **C** Titania and her servants are coming any minute.
- [ ] **D** The King of the Fairies is on his way.
- [ ] **E** The elves are coming to find her.

10 What does William Shakespeare seek to portray in the fairy's speech? Select the best option.

- [ ] **A** That the life of a fairy is hard
- [ ] **B** That nature is magical
- [ ] **C** That fairies argue
- [ ] **D** That most fairies come out at night
- [ ] **E** That fairies exist in reality

(11) What is the best synonym for the word "revels"? (line 18)
- [ ] **A** Fairy court
- [ ] **B** Tournament
- [ ] **C** Entertainment
- [ ] **D** Partygoers
- [ ] **E** Treats

(12) Why does Puck warn the fairy "Oberon is passing fell and wrath"?
- [ ] **A** The Fairy King is passing by soon.
- [ ] **B** The Fairy King is in a cruel and angry mood.
- [ ] **C** Oberon does not want to see the Queen.
- [ ] **D** The Queen has upset him.
- [ ] **E** Puck is afraid of Oberon.

(13) What have the Fairy King and Queen argued about?
- [ ] **A** An Indian king
- [ ] **B** A knight
- [ ] **C** A child
- [ ] **D** An elf
- [ ] **E** A meeting

(14) What part of the speech is the old-fashioned word "hath"? (line 21)
- [ ] **A** A past tense verb
- [ ] **B** A present tense verb
- [ ] **C** A preposition
- [ ] **D** A pronoun
- [ ] **E** An article

(15) What's the best definition of a "changeling"? (line 23)
- [ ] **A** A beautiful baby in fairyland
- [ ] **B** A child stolen by fairies
- [ ] **C** A child capable of causing jealousy amongst fairies
- [ ] **D** A baby treated as an attendant to the Fairy Queen
- [ ] **E** A child who steals fairy babies

(16) What would Oberon like to have the changeling for?
- [ ] **A** To be the King's companion in the forest
- [ ] **B** To be in command of Oberon's fairy train
- [ ] **C** To help him map out the unchartered forest
- [ ] **D** To take him to India
- [ ] **E** To force the queen into settling their argument

(17) What is the best modern translation of "perforce"? (line 26)
- [ ] **A** Forcibly
- [ ] **B** Possibly
- [ ] **C** Performance
- [ ] **D** Ferociously
- [ ] **E** Perhaps

(18) "Now they never meet in grove or green,
By fountain clear, or spangled starlight sheen"
What literacy feature is used here?

- [ ] **A** A metaphor
- [ ] **B** A simile
- [ ] **C** Personification
- [ ] **D** Onomatopoeia
- [ ] **E** Alliteration

(19) Why do the elves "creep into acorn cups"?

- [ ] **A** To look for acorns in the forest
- [ ] **B** To hide acorns under leaves
- [ ] **C** Because it frightens them to hear the King and Queen arguing
- [ ] **D** Because they are hiding from the King and Queen
- [ ] **E** Because they use acorn cups as drinking vessels

(20) What do Puck and the fairy discover during their conversation? That their quarrelling King and Queen...

- [ ] **A** have made friends
- [ ] **B** will never see each other again
- [ ] **C** will meet unexpectedly that night
- [ ] **D** are planning a party together
- [ ] **E** have frightened an Indian prince

In this book, there are extracts from different stories and plays. If you liked the passage, try to read the full version.

BILLY'S SHAKESPEAREAN SYNONYMS

In *A Midsummer Night's Dream* many archaic (old-fashioned) words are used. Use the text to help you try to match the Shakespearian language with the correct definition.

Shakespearian word	Definition
brier	has
anon	an ugly, stupid or strange child left by fairies in a place of a pretty, charming child
wrath	to what place or state
hath	cover with small sparkling objects
whither	soon; shortly
doth	tangled mass of prickly plants
changeling	does
spangled	extreme anger

Can you find any other archaic words used in the passage? Below are some words to investigate.

ere _____

fain _____

hark _____

hence _____

hie _____

thither _____

thee _____

thou _____

whence _____

Many words used during Shakespeare's day either have different meanings today or have been nearly forgotten. Can you use one in conversation?

11. JOURNEY TO THE CENTRE OF THE EARTH

1   He received me into his study; a perfect museum, containing every natural curiosity that can well be imagined - minerals, however, predominating. Every one was familiar to me having been catalogued by my own hand. My uncle, apparently oblivious of the fact that he had summoned me to his presence, was absorbed in a book. He was particularly fond

5   of early editions, tall copies and unique works.

"Wonderful!" he cried, tapping his forehead. "Wonderful – wonderful!"

It was one of those yellow-leaved volumes now rarely found on stalls, and to me it appeared to possess but little value. My uncle, however, was in raptures.

He admired its binding, the clearness of its characters, the ease with which it opened in his

10   hand, and repeated aloud, half a dozen times, that it was very, very old.

To my fancy he was making a great fuss about nothing but it was not my province to say so. On the contrary, I professed considerable interest in the subject and asked him what it was about.

"It is the Heims-Kringla of Snorre Tarleson," he said, "the celebrated Icelandic author

15   of the twelfth century – it is a true and correct account of the Norwegian princess who reigned in Iceland."

My next question related to the language in which it was written. I hoped at all events it was translated into German. My uncle was indignant at the very thought, and declared he wouldn't give a penny for a translation. His delight was to have found the original

20   work in the Icelandic tongue, which he declared to be one of the most magnificent and yet simple idioms in the world – while at the same time its grammatical combinations were the most varied known to students.

"About as easy as German?" was my insidious remark.

My uncle shrugged his shoulders.

25   "The letters in all events," I said, "are rather difficult of comprehension."

"It is a Runic manuscript, the language of the original population of Iceland, invented by Odin himself," cried my uncle, angry at my ignorance.

I was about to venture upon some misplaced joke on the subject, when a small scrap of parchment fell out of the leaves. Like a hungry man snatching at a morsel of bread the

30   professor seized it. It was about five inches by three and was scrawled over in the most extraordinary fashion.

The lines shown here are an exact facsimile of what was written on the venerable piece or parchment — and have wonderful importance, as they induced my uncle to undertake 34 the most wonderful series of adventures which ever fell to the lot of human beings.

Remember, if you do not know the meaning of a word, you can sometimes work it out by looking at how it works in its context.

II. A JOURNEY TO THE CENTRE OF THE EARTH
questions

(1) Why was the professor described as "Like a hungry man snatching at a morsel of bread"? (line 29)

- [ ] **A** He hadn't yet had lunch and was hungry.
- [ ] **B** He was rude and liked to snatch things without asking.
- [ ] **C** He was desperate to see what was on the paper.
- [ ] **D** He mistook the piece of paper for something else.

(2) What is the best synonym for "indignant"? (line 18)

- [ ] **A** Excited
- [ ] **B** Annoyed
- [ ] **C** Happy
- [ ] **D** Sad

(3) What was the professor was reading about? (lines 13–15)

- [ ] **A** A Norwegian princess
- [ ] **B** An Icelandic author
- [ ] **C** The twelfth century
- [ ] **D** A fictional story

(4) How was the professor's study described? (line 1)

- [ ] **A** Neat and tidy
- [ ] **B** A quiet library
- [ ] **C** A perfect museum
- [ ] **D** A clean laboratory

(5) What type of literary device is used in "Like a hungry man snatching at a morsel of bread"? (line 29)

- [ ] **A** Onomatopoeia
- [ ] **B** Personification
- [ ] **C** Simile
- [ ] **D** Metaphor

(6) What language did the boy hope the text was written in? (lines 17–18)

- [ ] **A** German
- [ ] **B** Icelandic
- [ ] **C** English
- [ ] **D** Dutch

7. Which two adjectives do you think most accurately describe the relationship between the boy and the professor?
- [ ] **A** Loving and caring
- [ ] **B** Affectionate and adoring
- [ ] **C** Dysfunctional and unstable
- [ ] **D** Educational and formal

8. Why did the author use the word "summoned" to describe how the boy came to be in the professor's study? (line 4)
- [ ] **A** The study was a scary place to be and the boy was afraid of the professor.
- [ ] **B** The boy was in trouble and had no choice but to go.
- [ ] **C** It is a better verb than 'called'.
- [ ] **D** The word 'summoned' is a formal verb and reflects their relationship.

9. Which of the following words best describe how the professor felt about the book he was reading?
- [ ] **A** Bored and unengaged
- [ ] **B** Baffled and confused
- [ ] **C** Engaged and excited
- [ ] **D** Amused and tickled

10. What type of writing is this passage?
- [ ] **A** Second person non-fiction
- [ ] **B** First person fiction
- [ ] **C** Third person fiction
- [ ] **D** First person non-fiction

11. What did the professor like about the book that he was reading? (lines 9–10)
- [ ] **A** The vagueness of the characters
- [ ] **B** The contemporary story line
- [ ] **C** The binding
- [ ] **D** The difficulty he had in opening it

12. Which word below is an antonym for "fond"? (line 4)
- [ ] **A** Compassionate
- [ ] **B** Selfish
- [ ] **C** Empathetic
- [ ] **D** Uncaring

13. What did the professor do while he was reading the book? (line 6)
- [ ] **A** Tapped his forehead
- [ ] **B** Twiddled his fingers
- [ ] **C** Tapped his feet
- [ ] **D** Squinted his eyes

(14) What does "yellow-leaved volumes" imply? (line 7)
- [ ] **A** The book was printed on yellow paper.
- [ ] **B** The book looked like leaves on a tree.
- [ ] **C** The book was very old.
- [ ] **D** The book was not very nice.

(15) Why do you think the boy showed interest in the book when he was not really interested?
- [ ] **A** He was afraid of the professor.
- [ ] **B** He didn't want to seem impolite.
- [ ] **C** He wanted to know more about the old book.
- [ ] **D** He was not very educated.

(16) Why did the author use the word "cried" to describe the way the professor spoke to the boy? (line 27)
- [ ] **A** The professor was tearful.
- [ ] **B** The professor was speaking quietly.
- [ ] **C** The professor was frustrated.
- [ ] **D** The professor was talking in a level voice.

(17) Why would the professor not give a penny for a translation of the text? (line 19)
- [ ] **A** He was poor and didn't want to waste money.
- [ ] **B** He didn't trust the translation.
- [ ] **C** He thought a translation would be worth much more than that.
- [ ] **D** He appreciated the language it was written in.

(18) Which two words would best describe the professor?
i) intelligent   ii) uneducated   iii) mean   iv) educated
- [ ] **A** i and iv
- [ ] **B** iv and ii
- [ ] **C** i and iii
- [ ] **D** ii and iii

(19) Why did the author use the adjective "misplaced" to describe the boy's joke? (line 28)
- [ ] **A** The joke would have been appreciated by his uncle.
- [ ] **B** The joke was not suitable for the situation.
- [ ] **C** The joke would have been better earlier in the conversation.
- [ ] **D** The joke was not funny.

(20) What type of word is the word "translated"? (line 18)
- [ ] **A** A noun
- [ ] **B** An adjective
- [ ] **C** An adverb
- [ ] **D** A verb

BILLY'S INCREDIBLE IDIOMS

What is an idiom? An idiom is a word or phrase which means something different from its literal (actual) meaning. They might seem confusing at first, but most idioms were born hundreds of years ago and have become part of everyday English speech. Can you complete these common idioms? Underneath each one write the true translation.

1. **That costs an _____ and a leg.**

    _____

2. **Break a _____.**

    _____

3. **Piece of _____.**

    _____

4. **Takes _____ to tango.**

    _____

5. **'Up in the _____.'**

    _____

6. **Kill two birds with one _____.**

    _____

7. **Rule of _____.**

    _____

8. **Blow off _____.**

    _____

Learning these idioms can help you become skilled in the English language. See if you can find more idioms and start using them in conversations.

12. A NEW START

1   There once was a mouse who enjoyed sneaking,
    From around alley corners he loved peeking.
    He was the sneakiest mouse around about town,
    And when people discovered him, he was met with some frowns.
5   The frowns were accompanied by screams and some shrieks,
    And it took ladies some time to recover, some weeks.

    The cute little mouse couldn't fathom out why,
    Just his appearance would make people cry,
    And that is the reason he chose to be sneaky,
10 He crawled through dark sewage pipes that were often quite leaky.
    It was a horrible life to keep sneaking around,
    Hoping that he would never be found.

    Until one fine day he met a pigeon named Sue.
    She said, "Escape city life!" then away quickly she flew.
15 The mouse pondered a while, he'd never considered a move,
    And needed some time to think it all through,
    Because moving out of the city meant untangling his roots,
    And packing all of his stuff, including his boots.

    A few short weeks later, enough was enough,
20 And he decided to leave even though it was tough,.
    So he packed his small bag and slung it over his back,
    And grabbed some food from his cupboards to have as a snack.
    Then off he adventured into the wild.
    As he was leaving the city, he waved and he smiled.
25 He had a good feeling about his new start in life,
    He had an inkling he'd live with minimum strife.

    After a few hours of scuttling along,
    His iPpod was playing all his favourite songs.
    It helped him to feel somewhat upbeat,
30 And to stop him from worrying about the sores on his feet.
    But he felt slightly anxious as he scrambled over the wall,
    He had lived in the city, since he was very small.
    But you should never feel worried about the unknown,
    Because excitement and adventure are found outside the home.

35 Eventually the concrete faded to grass.
    The little mouse sighed and whispered softly, "At last . . ."
    His small feet were tickled by the long blades of green,
    And the scenery around him was the most stunning he'd seen.
    There in the distance he could see the tallest of trees,

40 And surrounding the flowers he heard the buzzing of bees.
   These sounds had replaced the noise of the city,
   And this significant change was by no means a pity.
   "How wonderful it is to find somewhere new and so nice,
   It would make me so happy to find a family of mice."

45 And just at that moment as if his wish had come true,
   He heard little voices shouting, "We're coming through!"
   Five little mice came running past at some speed,
   With the biggest of mice who was taking the lead.
   So our little mouse followed the mouse conga train,
50 And never returned to the city again.

   So if you're ever afraid to try something new,
52 Give it a go – you may discover a new you.

   By Lauren Pusey

Remember to read the question with great care. Misreading or not reading even a small word can change the question.

12. A NEW START questions

① What is the moral of this poem?
- [ ] **A** Being different is OK.
- [ ] **B** Never be afraid to do new things.
- [ ] **C** Cities are not very nice places to be.
- [ ] **D** People in the countryside are friendly and welcoming.

② What is an antonym for "fathom"? (line 7)
- [ ] **A** Understand
- [ ] **B** Perceive
- [ ] **C** Cognise
- [ ] **D** Misinterpret

③ Which best describes the way that the poet feels about the mouse?
- [ ] **A** She feels the mouse is a dirty creature.
- [ ] **B** She feels sympathetic towards to the mouse
- [ ] **C** She feels indifferent towards the mouse.
- [ ] **D** She dislikes the mouse.

④ Which best describes what 'an inkling' is? (line 26)
- [ ] **A** A small suspicion
- [ ] **B** An important thought
- [ ] **C** A small patch of ink
- [ ] **D** A strong feeling of emotion

⑤ How did people feel about the mouse?
- [ ] **A** They thought he was cute.
- [ ] **B** They were scared of him.
- [ ] **C** They felt indifferent.
- [ ] **D** They wanted to keep him as a pet.

⑥ Where was the mouse happiest?
- [ ] **A** Stanza 1
- [ ] **B** Stanza 4
- [ ] **C** Stanza 6
- [ ] **D** Stanza 5

⑦ Why did the mouse decide to leave the city?
- [ ] **A** The pigeon told him to.
- [ ] **B** He had heard wonderful things about the countryside.
- [ ] **C** He wanted to see if he could have a nicer life.
- [ ] **D** He wanted to visit his friends.

(8) Why did the mouse sneak around?

- [ ] **A** He enjoyed making people jump.
- [ ] **B** He wanted to be invisible.
- [ ] **C** He didn't want to be seen.
- [ ] **D** He wasn't very sociable.

(9) Who was at the back of the mouse conga train?

- [ ] **A** The biggest mouse
- [ ] **B** The smallest mouse
- [ ] **C** We don't know.
- [ ] **D** The main mouse in the story

(10) What type of word is "tickled"? (line 37)

- [ ] **A** An adjective
- [ ] **B** A verb
- [ ] **C** A noun
- [ ] **D** An adverb

(11) What is a synonym for "pondered"? (line 15)

- [ ] **A** Deliberated
- [ ] **B** Pondered
- [ ] **C** Suggested
- [ ] **D** Lake

(12) Does the poet think that the people are justified in being afraid of the mouse?

- [ ] **A** Yes, because mice are dirty creatures.
- [ ] **B** No, because he is a cute little mouse.
- [ ] **C** Yes, because he sneaks up on people.
- [ ] **D** No, because he is gentle and won't harm anyone.

(13) Why do you think the mouse had to think about the move?

- [ ] **A** He had heard negative things about the countryside.
- [ ] **B** He was afraid of the unknown.
- [ ] **C** He had only ever lived in the city.
- [ ] **D** He wasn't very good at making decisions.

(14) In the sixth stanza, what is the mood of the poem?

- [ ] **A** The poet has created a tranquil mood.
- [ ] **B** The poet intends the reader to feel anxious.
- [ ] **C** There is a feeling of sadness.
- [ ] **D** The mood to the stanza is ecstatic excitement.

(15) What does the word "upbeat" describe? (line 29)

- [ ] **A** The music the mouse was listening to
- [ ] **B** The general feeling of the stanza
- [ ] **C** The mouse's emotions
- [ ] **D** The way the mouse was moving

16 How many syllables are there in line 4?

    A   15

    B   14

    C   11

    D   13

17 What does the word "strife" mean? (line 26)

    A   Conflict

    B   Happiness

    C   Sadness

    D   Devastation

18 What is another word for "untangling"? (line 17)

    A   Tangle

    B   Intertwine

    C   Unsnarl

    D   Unaltered

19 What sounds replaced the noise of the city? (stanza 6)

    A   The singing of birds

    B   The hooting of cars

    C   The buzzing of bees

    D   The rustling of leaves in the tree

20 Which word would best describe the mouse at the end of the poem?

    A   Content

    B   Sad

    C   Apprehensive

    D   Ecstatic

BILLY'S PERFECT PERSONIFICATION

Personification is a literacy device we use to give human characteristics to things. It can often be found in poetry. This device can give deeper meaning and aid understanding. Below are some examples of how personification can be used in a sentence.

1.   **Opportunity knocked on his door.**

2.   **Jamie's alarm clock screams at him every morning.**

3.   **The stairs moaned as they walked on them.**

4.   **The waves devoured the grains of sand on the beach.**

5.   **The book was so popular, it flew off the shelves.**

6.   **The errors leapt off the page when Julia reviewed her homework.**

Below, can you write a sentence using personification that relates to each topic word?

Sport

_____

Animals

_____

Weather

_____

Vehicles

_____

The main purpose of personification is to bring inanimate things to life, to better explain them. It is easier for us to relate to something that is human.

13. ANTS

1 Ants are insects with six legs and bodies that are divided into three main parts: the head, thorax and abdomen. They hatch from eggs into legless grubs and when they are grown they turn into pupae. From the pupae state, the ants grow into fully formed ants and this process is known as metamorphosis. There are over 10,000 species of ant and as many
5 as 10,000 trillion ants alive at any one time in the world.

Colonies

Ants are very social animals and they live in colonies that are made up of different types of ants with very specific jobs. The colonies are like towns and they can consist of several million ants. Different types of ants build their colonies in different places. African weaver
10 ants live in the treetops whereas tiny trapjaw ants live in small colonies inside split twigs. Most ants' nests have complicated structures and there are various chambers that they use at different times of the day. Some chambers are purely where the ants store their rubbish while others are used for egg storage. Some ants even build tunnels to allow air to enter and leave the nest, which act as an air conditioning system. During the winter
15 months, the ants will use the chambers further down in the nest where it is less frosty; in the summer they will use the chambers near the surface.

Different types of ants

There are three main types of ants in a colony: the queen (or queens), the female workers and the males. There are also soldier ants which are a type of worker whose
20 main job is to protect the queen and other workers and also bring back food. The majority of ants in a colony are worker ants and they are all wingless and female. Unlike most other animals, the female workers do not reproduce but rather they gather food, build the nest, care for the eggs and feed the queen ant. The queen is responsible for all new life in the colony. She is the largest ant and has a larger abdomen than the other
25 ants because she lays all the eggs. The queen will only mate once because she is able to store the male cells in her abdomen and they will last her lifetime. She is able to lay an egg every two seconds and over a lifespan of ten years can produce 150 million daughter worker ants. Male ants are generally smaller than the queen and their task is to fly away and mate with other queens.

30 **Food**

Most ants are predators and they catch and eat other insects and invertebrates. Often ants will work as a team to capture larger prey, so that they can overcome insects that are larger than they are. A colony of wood ants can gather up to 100,000 caterpillars in just one day. They, like most animals, need a supply of water and some ants carry water droplets to
35 the nest between their jaws. When they return to the nest, ants will feed the other ants in the nest by vomiting some of what they have eaten into the other ants' mouths.

Although ants are predators, they are very low on the food chain and so a lot of animals would enjoy a feast on them. Armadillos, ant eaters and woodpeckers are just some of the animals that search out ants to eat. Ant eaters have special sticky tongues that
40 allow them to eat several ants at a time and reach deep into the nests. Some people in the Philippines and Australia enjoy snacking on ants.

Always read the whole passage, do not skim and scan. This is important to ensure you don't miss any important sentences.

13. ANTS questions

1. What is a synonym for "metamorphosis"? (line 4)
   - [ ] **A** Growth
   - [ ] **B** Transformation
   - [ ] **C** Stagnation
   - [ ] **D** Activity

2. What is the name of the place where the ants live?
   - [ ] **A** Nest
   - [ ] **B** Home
   - [ ] **C** Colony
   - [ ] **D** Chambers

3. What type of animals are ants?
   - [ ] **A** Insects
   - [ ] **B** Reptiles
   - [ ] **C** Mammals
   - [ ] **D** None of the above

4. How many ants are alive at any given time in the world?
   - [ ] **A** 10,000
   - [ ] **B** 10,000 million
   - [ ] **C** 100,000
   - [ ] **D** 10,000 trillion

5. Why do ants use the lower chambers in the winter?
   - [ ] **A** Because it is warmer further down
   - [ ] **B** Because they hibernate in the warmth
   - [ ] **C** Because they want to hide from predators
   - [ ] **D** Because they don't like the winter

6. Which ants are the largest in the colony?
   - [ ] **A** The worker ants
   - [ ] **B** The soldier ants
   - [ ] **C** The males
   - [ ] **D** The queens

7. What do the male ants do?
   - [ ] **A** Forage for food
   - [ ] **B** Protect the queen
   - [ ] **C** Mate with other queen ants
   - [ ] **D** Nothing

⑧ How many caterpillars can ants gather in one day?
☐ **A** 10,000
☐ **B** 1000
☐ **C** 100,000
☐ **D** 100

⑨ Why do ants build extra tunnels in their colonies? (lines 13–14)
☐ **A** So they can move in and out of them.
☐ **B** So they let air in and out of the colony.
☐ **C** So they have more than one escape route if predators try to eat them.
☐ **D** There is no reason.

⑩ What is a synonym for "mate"? (line 25)
☐ **A** Friend
☐ **B** Enemy
☐ **C** Reproduce
☐ **D** Comrade

⑪ What are the female ants not responsible for? (lines 22–23)
☐ **A** Laying eggs
☐ **B** Gathering food
☐ **C** Building the colony
☐ **D** Protecting the colony

⑫ What feature helps ant eaters to catch the ants? (line 39)
☐ **A** Their eyesight
☐ **B** Their speed
☐ **C** Their sticky tongues
☐ **D** Their long tongues

⑬ What is a synonym for "various"? (line 11)
☐ **A** Different
☐ **B** Few
☐ **C** Limited
☐ **D** Scarce

⑭ Which of the following statements is not true about ants?
☐ **A** They drink water.
☐ **B** They always live underground.
☐ **C** They live in groups.
☐ **D** They can fly.

⑮ Why might ant eaters need long tongues?
☐ **A** So that they can reach up high.
☐ **B** So that they use them to feel out ants to eat.
☐ **C** So that they can reach into ant colonies.
☐ **D** So that they don't have very good eyesight.

(16) What does being a "predator" mean? (lines 31 and 37)

☐ **A** You are eaten by other animals.
☐ **B** You eat other animals.
☐ **C** You eat only plants.
☐ **D** None of the above

(17) How do the ants feed the other ants in the nest? (lines 35–36)

☐ **A** They put it into the food storage chamber.
☐ **B** They carry the food back in their jaws.
☐ **C** They regurgitate the food.
☐ **D** They drop the food into the nest.

(18) What type of word is the word "care" in this sentence from the text? "Unlike most other animals the female workers do not reproduce but rather they gather food, build the nest, care for the eggs and feed the queen ant." (lines 21–23)

☐ **A** An adjective
☐ **B** A noun
☐ **C** A preposition
☐ **D** A verb

(19) What might the "abdomen" be responsible for? (line 26)

☐ **A** Digestion
☐ **B** Reproduction
☐ **C** Respiration
☐ **D** Excretion

(20) In what countries does the author suggest that ants are eaten?

☐ **A** Africa and India
☐ **B** Africa and Philippines
☐ **C** Papua New Guinea
☐ **D** Philippines and Australia

BILLY'S SUPER STATISTICS

Facts are not what you feel or think – they are true pieces of information. The comprehension titled 'Ants' contains lots of facts and figures. Can you find the facts in the passage that link to the following numbers?

1. **Six**

   _____

2. **Ten thousand**

   _____

3. **One hundred and fifty million**

   _____

4. **One hundred thousand**

   _____

5. **Two seconds**

   _____

6. **Ten thousand trillion**

   _____

In the above task, you needed to find a piece of information. This important skill of scanning the text is vitally important when answering comprehension questions. If you found it challenging, look for key words that will help you discover that information quickly.

Referring back to the text is useful to help support your ideas. Don't feel you need to remember everything – the answers are somewhere in the text!

14. BLACK BEAUTY

1   Before I was two years old a circumstance happened which I have never forgotten. It was early in the spring; there had been a little frost in the night, and a light mist still hung over the woods and meadows. I and the other colts were feeding at the lower part of the field when we heard, quite in the distance, what sounded like the cry of dogs. The oldest of the

5   colts raised his head, pricked his ears, and said, "There are the hounds!" and immediately cantered off, followed by the rest of us to the upper part of the field, where we could look over the hedge and see several fields beyond. My mother and an old riding horse of our master's were also standing near, and seemed to know all about it.

  "They have found a hare," said my mother, "and if they come this way we shall see the

10   hunt."

  And soon the dogs were all tearing down the field of young wheat next to ours. I never heard such a noise as they made. They did not bark, nor howl, nor whine, but kept on a "Yo! Yo, o, o! Yo! Yo, o, o!" at the top of their voices. After them came a number of men on horseback, some of them in green coats, all galloping as fast as they could. The

15   old horse snorted and looked eagerly after them, and we young colts wanted to be galloping with them, but they were soon away into the fields lower down; here it seemed as if they had come to a stand; the dogs left off barking, and ran about every way with their noses to the ground.

  "They have lost the scent," said the old horse; "perhaps the hare will get off."

20   "What hare?" I said.

  "Oh! I don't know what hare; likely enough it may be one of our own hares out of the woods; any hare they can find will do for the dogs and men to run after;" and before long the dogs began their "Yo! Yo, o, o!" again, and back they came altogether at full speed, making straight for our meadow at the part where the high bank and hedge

25   overhang the brook.

  "Now we shall see the hare," said my mother; and just then a hare wild with fright rushed by and made for the woods. On came the dogs; they burst over the bank, leaped the stream, and came dashing across the field followed by the huntsmen. Six or eight men leaped their horses clean over, close upon the dogs. The hare tried to get through

30   the fence; it was too thick, and she turned sharp round to make for the road, but it was too late; the dogs were upon her with their wild cries; we heard one shriek, and that was the end of her. One of the huntsmen rode up and whipped off the dogs, who would soon have torn her to pieces. He held her up by the leg torn and bleeding, and all the gentlemen seemed well pleased.

35   As for me, I was so astonished that I did not at first see what was going on by the brook; but when I did look there was a sad sight; two fine horses were down, one was

struggling in the stream, and the other was groaning on the grass. One of the riders was getting out of the water covered with mud, the other lay quite still.

"His neck is broke," said my mother.

40 "And serve him right, too," said one of the colts.

I thought the same, but my mother did not join with us.

"Well, no," she said, "you must not say that; but though I am an old horse, and have seen and heard a great deal, I never yet could make out why men are so fond of this sport; they often hurt themselves, often spoil good horses, and tear up the fields, and all
45 for a hare or a fox, or a stag, that they could get more easily some other way; but we are only horses, and don't know."

While my mother was saying this we stood and looked on. Many of the riders had gone to the young man; but my master, who had been watching what was going on, was the first to raise him. His head fell back and his arms hung down, and everyone looked very
50 serious. There was no noise now; even the dogs were quiet, and seemed to know that something was wrong. They carried him to our master's house. I heard afterward that it was young George Gordon, the squire's only son, a fine, tall young man, and the pride of
53 his family.

While answering the comprehension questions, always refer back to the passage to clarify your answer.

14. BLACK BEAUTY questions

(1) Who is narrating the story?

- [ ] **A** A little boy
- [ ] **B** A little girl
- [ ] **C** The horse
- [ ] **D** The mother

(2) What did the mother think about the hunt of the hare? (lines 42–46)

- [ ] **A** She thought that it was wrong.
- [ ] **B** She thought it was fine and had no problem.
- [ ] **C** She enjoyed hunting herself.
- [ ] **D** She thought it was not her place to say.

(3) What does it mean when the author says that the young colt "pricked his ears"? (line 5)

- [ ] **A** He was listening to what was going on.
- [ ] **B** He flapped his ears around.
- [ ] **C** He couldn't hear very well.
- [ ] **D** He was frustrated that he couldn't hear.

(4) What is a "colt"? (line 3)

- [ ] **A** A young dog
- [ ] **B** A young horse
- [ ] **C** A young hare
- [ ] **D** A young deer

(5) How old was Black Beauty when he witnessed the hunt?

- [ ] **A** 1 year old
- [ ] **B** 2 years old
- [ ] **C** 5 years old
- [ ] **D** An adult

(6) Why do you think that Black Beauty had never forgotten what he saw that day?

- [ ] **A** He was excited and wanted to join in.
- [ ] **B** He was traumatised by what he saw, and so it stuck with him.
- [ ] **C** He has a good memory.
- [ ] **D** He enjoyed watching the hunt and watched many more after that.

(7) What is an antonym for "dashing"? (line 28)

- [ ] **A** Rushing
- [ ] **B** Dawdling
- [ ] **C** Skipping
- [ ] **D** Sprinting

⑧ What month could the hunt have taken place in? (line 2)

- [ ] **A** December
- [ ] **B** August
- [ ] **C** October
- [ ] **D** March

⑨ Why did the oldest colt canter off? (lines 5–7)

- [ ] **A** He wanted to see the hunt.
- [ ] **B** He enjoyed cantering because he could go fast.
- [ ] **C** He was afraid of the sound of the hounds.
- [ ] **D** He was uninterested in the hunt.

⑩ Why does the author use a lot of exclamation marks? (line 13)

- [ ] **A** They are better than using full stops.
- [ ] **B** Using exclamation marks has no effect on the text.
- [ ] **C** The horse was excited to see what was going on.
- [ ] **D** It shows that the noise was loud.

⑪ What did Black Beauty think about the hunt? (lines 41–46)

- [ ] **A** It is a good sport.
- [ ] **B** It is a dangerous and silly sport.
- [ ] **C** It is exciting and enjoyable.
- [ ] **D** He felt indifferent.

⑫ What type of word is "burst" in this sentence from the text? "On came the dogs; they burst over the bank, leaped the stream, and came dashing across the field followed by the huntsmen." (lines 27–28)

- [ ] **A** An adjective
- [ ] **B** An adverb
- [ ] **C** A verb
- [ ] **D** A noun

⑬ Why did the dogs go quiet after the boy had fallen from the horse? (lines 50–51)

- [ ] **A** They were hungry and tired.
- [ ] **B** They were told to be quiet.
- [ ] **C** They sensed something was wrong.
- [ ] **D** They were eating.

⑭ What is a synonym for "fond"? (line 43)

- [ ] **A** Uncaring
- [ ] **B** Loving
- [ ] **C** Indifferent
- [ ] **D** Excited

(15) How did the boy get hurt?

- [ ] **A**   He fell from his horse when his horse tried to jump the stream.
- [ ] **B**   He fell over when he was running after the hounds.
- [ ] **C**   He wasn't hurt.
- [ ] **D**   We don't know.

(16) What type of word is the word "by" in this sentence from the text? 'I did not at first see what was going on by the brook.' (line 35)

- [ ] **A**   An article
- [ ] **B**   An adjective
- [ ] **C**   A verb
- [ ] **D**   A preposition

(17) What did the horses mean when they said "They have lost the scent"? (line 19)

- [ ] **A**   The dogs couldn't smell the horses.
- [ ] **B**   The dogs couldn't smell the people.
- [ ] **C**   The dogs couldn't smell the hare.
- [ ] **D**   The dogs couldn't smell the flowers.

(18) What does the phrase "spoil good horses" mean? (line 44)

- [ ] **A**   Horses get injured.
- [ ] **B**   Horses get lots of treats when they are good.
- [ ] **C**   Give your horse lots of apples.
- [ ] **D**   Horses get spoiled with nice things when they hunt.

(19) How many horses had fallen?

- [ ] **A**   One
- [ ] **B**   None
- [ ] **C**   Two
- [ ] **D**   Five

(20) What type of horse was Black Beauty's mother? (line 7)

- [ ] **A**   A race horse
- [ ] **B**   We don't know.
- [ ] **C**   A wild horse
- [ ] **D**   A riding horse

BILLY'S OBLIGING ONOMATOPOEIAS

In the *Black Beauty* extract there are many words used to describe the sound made by the different animals mentioned e.g. "bark" or "shriek". Onomatopoeia is words that imitate, resemble or suggest the source of the sound they describe. Common occurrences of the word of the onomatopoeia process include animal noises such as "oink" or "miaow". Onomatopoeia appeals to the sense of hearing and in the previous comprehension it is used to bring the story to life. Below, can you write an animal that might make the sound? In some cases there might be more than one animal.

1. bleat   _____

2. bray   _____

3. caw   _____

4. cluck   _____

5. bell   _____

6. croak   _____

7. roar   _____

8. coo   _____

9. gobble   _____

10. click   _____

Onomatopoeias is often used in poetry. These words sound like what they mean e.g. "thud", "crash", "bang" and "buzz". Can you think of any more and record them below?

_____

_____

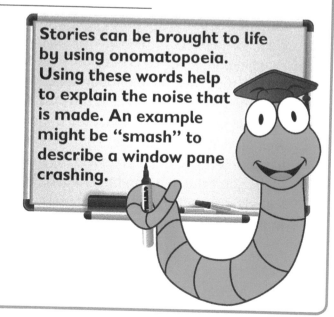

Stories can be brought to life by using onomatopoeia. Using these words help to explain the noise that is made. An example might be "smash" to describe a window pane crashing.

15. DEFORESTATION

1 Deforestation is the clearing and removal of trees from an area without the intention of
replanting them. It has been a particularly hot topic in recent years as deforestation not
only has a huge impact on the ecosystems living in the forests, but it is also considered
to be a major cause of global warming. Every year rainforests the size of England are
5 being cleared for a variety of reasons.

Shockingly, around 17–20% of the Amazon Rainforest has been lost in the past 50 years,
which is a devastating figure. If deforestation continues at this rapid rate, it could have
catastrophic consequences for future generations. Not only will future generations be
unable to experience the diverse wildlife within the rainforests, but deforestation could
10 have more serious implications for the state of our planet.

Why are rainforests so important?

Rainforests are an essential part of the Earth's ecosystem. Over 80% of all the Earth's
animals can be found in the rainforests. In 2014, three hundred and eighty-one new
species of animals and plants were discovered in the Amazon Rainforest, which is a truly
15 amazing figure.

Trees are also very important as they absorb greenhouse gases which, in turn, reduce
the risk of global warming. They use up carbon dioxide and produce oxygen. Trees also
help with the water cycle by returning vapour to the air. In addition to the benefits that
the rainforest has on various animals and the environment, there are around 1.6 billion
20 people who rely on rainforests for food, clothing, medicine, water and shelter. These
indigenous people populate remote areas of the rainforest and are barely touched by
civilisation. For them, the rainforest provides all of their needs including providing all the
food and shelter that they require.

How and why does deforestation happen?

25 One of the primary causes for rainforests being cut down is agriculture. Many farmers
clear large parts of the rainforests for grazing their livestock, planting crops and cattle
ranching. In order to create an environment that is suitable for farming, they need to
ensure that they have enough space to plant crops and to give them the amount of light
that they need to grow and also they need space for the livestock to graze and roam.
30 Palm oil is an ingredient in a lot of household products including cosmetics and foods, as
well as cleaning products. This oil is obtained from the trees in the rainforest and is used
irresponsibly in many products. In some cases, it is hard to find replacements for palm
oil but, in others, it can be avoided. The wood from the trees is used for many purposes
including making furniture and paper. The high demand for both of these commodities
35 makes it hard to source the wood without a negative impact on the environment.

Illegal logging can be another big problem because there are many people who cut down trees without permission. This not only means that the companies are taking resources that do not belong to them, but they are also profiting more because they are not paying the relevant fees for the resources. Furthermore, around 15% of all emissions
40 result from deforestation, which is a staggering figure when car and factory emissions are taken into consideration. This damages the environment even more.
Finally, wildfire is one of the biggest causes of deforestation. It is natural and, sadly, unavoidable.

How can we help?

45 There are many ways in which we can assist in preventing deforestation. One of the ways that large corporations can help is by balancing the trees that are cut down by planting new ones. On a smaller scale, individuals can help by using both sides of paper and recycling the paper they used. In addition, we can read more on-screen rather than printing; this includes newspapers as well as books and other printed materials.
50 Furthermore, when buying furniture that is made from wood, it is important to ensure that it is always certified wood and, therefore, that it has been cut down legally as opposed to illegally logged.

15. DEFORESTATION questions

1. Which is a synonym for "essential"? (line 12)
   - [ ] **A** Indispensable
   - [ ] **B** Unnecessary
   - [ ] **C** Ideal
   - [ ] **D** Unimportant

2. Name two things that we could do to help reduce deforestation. (lines 45–52)
   - [ ] **A** Use more palm oil products.
   - [ ] **B** Recycle more paper.
   - [ ] **C** Buy furniture not made from wood.
   - [ ] **D** Read more on-screen.

3. What does the author mean by "hot topic"? (line 2)
   - [ ] **A** Deforestation is causing global warming.
   - [ ] **B** People are very excited about deforestation.
   - [ ] **C** It has been widely discussed.
   - [ ] **D** It is just a saying with no meaning.

4. What type of word is the word "grazing"? (line 26)
   - [ ] **A** An adjective
   - [ ] **B** A verb
   - [ ] **C** A noun
   - [ ] **D** An adverb

5. According to the text, what percentage of emissions are not caused by deforestation? (lines 39–40)
   - [ ] **A** 15%
   - [ ] **B** 50%
   - [ ] **C** 85%
   - [ ] **D** 35%

6. If deforestation continues at the same rate as the last 50 years, how much of the Amazon Rainforest will be gone in the next 100 years? (line 6)
   - [ ] **A** 17%
   - [ ] **B** 44%
   - [ ] **C** 51%
   - [ ] **D** 34–40%

7. What product do we not get from the rainforest? (lines 30–35)
   - [ ] **A** Wood
   - [ ] **B** Paper
   - [ ] **C** Make-up
   - [ ] **D** Diamonds

⑧ What is a natural cause of deforestation?
- [ ] **A** Logging
- [ ] **B** Agriculture
- [ ] **C** Wildfire
- [ ] **D** None of the above

⑨ Which word best describes how the author feels about deforestation?
- [ ] **A** Indifferent
- [ ] **B** Concerned
- [ ] **C** Sad
- [ ] **D** Happy

⑩ What is "rapid rate" an example of? (line 7)
- [ ] **A** Alliteration
- [ ] **B** Personification
- [ ] **C** Sibilance
- [ ] **D** Pathetic fallacy

⑪ Why do farmers need to cut down trees?
- [ ] **A** Because wild animals live there
- [ ] **B** They need space to plant crops
- [ ] **C** The trees are hazardous
- [ ] **D** There is too much water in the rainforest

⑫ What does the word "indigenous" mean? (line 21)
- [ ] **A** People who live in an area
- [ ] **B** People who are native to an area
- [ ] **C** The first ever people on the Earth
- [ ] **D** People who don't belong there

⑬ What type of word is "essential" in this sentence from the text? "Rainforests are an essential part of the Earth's ecosystem." (line 12)
- [ ] **A** An adverb
- [ ] **B** A preposition
- [ ] **C** A noun
- [ ] **D** An adjective

⑭ Why might the author have included lots of figures in the text?
- [ ] **A** To ensure the reader knows the numbers.
- [ ] **B** To make the reader aware of the precise impact.
- [ ] **C** There is no logical reason.
- [ ] **D** Having numbers is better than words.

(15) What would not assist in the prevention of deforestation?
- [ ] **A** Recycling paper
- [ ] **B** Buying second-hand wooden furniture
- [ ] **C** Watching a documentary on deforestation
- [ ] **D** Not using products containing palm oil

(16) What would a permit allow the farmers to do?
- [ ] **A** To sell the wood from the trees
- [ ] **B** To cut down the trees legally
- [ ] **C** Stop deforestation
- [ ] **D** Grow more trees

(17) Which two words best summarise the tone of the passage?
- [ ] **A** Sombre and depressed
- [ ] **B** Excited and ambitious
- [ ] **C** Indifferent and unaffected
- [ ] **D** Concerned and informative

(18) What does the author feel future generations should be able to experience in rain forests? (lines 8–10)
- [ ] **A** Their beauty
- [ ] **B** Their many trees
- [ ] **C** Their impressive wildlife
- [ ] **D** Their water systems

(19) What is an antonym for "major"?
- [ ] **A** Minor
- [ ] **B** Significant
- [ ] **C** Important
- [ ] **D** Small

(20) How many new species of animals were found in a single year in the Amazon Rainforest?
- [ ] **A** Two thousand and fourteen
- [ ] **B** Two hundred and eighty
- [ ] **C** Five hundred and twelve
- [ ] **D** Three hundred and eighty-one

BILLY'S GRAND GLOSSARY

A glossary of terms can help understand difficult terminology used in a passage. Glossaries are presented in alphabetical order and use short, concise definitions. These words are often shown in **bold** so they can be easily identified. A list of words can be difficult to learn but it is worth it if you want to improve the vocabulary you use in your every day life. Look out for these words in your reading.

Using the words below, create a glossary based on the deforestation passage. Use a dictionary and remember to write your glossary in alphabetical order.

indigenous

ecosystem

commodities

civilisation

global warming

diverse

greenhouse gases

livestock

cosmetics

vapour

Can you have a conversation with an adult or friend using your glossary to warn them about deforestation?

16. FOREST

1 It was a cold wintry night. The trees were swaying and creaking and the branches reached out like spindly witches' fingers grabbing at the air. The whistling of the wind sounded like pitch pipes and a chill ran down Allegra's spine. She was accustomed to walking home from school through the woods but, as the days got shorter and the
5 nights grew darker, she felt less comfortable doing so. This particular night, the extreme weather conditions left Allegra feeling very uncomfortable. As she walked through the forest she quickened her pace until she was walking very briskly. She listened as the leaves rustled above her head and the twigs crackled and snapped under her feet. All the time she was focused on the lights coming from the streets in the distance. They seemed
10 like an oasis and she was desperate to reach them as soon as possible.

After what seemed like a lifetime, Allegra reached the street. She burst out of the frightening forest and into the warm cosy street lighting. Her mood immediately transformed as she felt safe and secure in the street where she had grown up. A few metres down the road she spotted her home and she couldn't wait to walk through the
15 door and be greeted by the wet nose and wagging tail of her best friend, Sidney. He had been part of the family for six years now, but still behaved as if he were only a few months old and bounded around with the same amount of enthusiasm. If only people were as friendly as Sidney, the world would be a better place, she thought to herself. He was happiness personified.

20 Things in Allegra's house worked like clockwork. Everything had a set time slot and there was never a spontaneous moment. Allegra often wondered what it would be like to live in a less ordered household. In her house everything had its own place and there was not a speck of dust in sight. She longed to live in a house where everything was more free-spirited. Her best friend Josie's house was the complete opposite of hers. Josie didn't
25 worry about what time she was home or if she had wiped the kitchen counters after she had made toast. It was bliss. Sadly this wasn't the case for Allegra. She glanced at the clock in the hallway and it showed five-thirty. Dad would be home in half an hour and dinner would be on the table. Allegra knew that, in the meantime, she would have had to have completed her homework and fed the dog, or risk her mother's wrath.

30 Being the dutiful daughter she was, she ensured all was done before dinner. Unfortunately, whatever she did never seemed to be enough. Her mother was always 'nit-picking' and this evening was no different. The dog had been fed and her homework was done but she had not made her bed in the morning and that alone seemed to cause her mother tremendous stress. Allegra was relieved when dinner was
35 over and she could escape to her room. Another day was done and she could relax in peace.

16. FOREST questions

1. What literary device has been used for "frightening forest"? (line 12)
   - A   Sibilance
   - B   Onomatopoeia
   - C   Alliteration
   - D   Simile

2. What literary device is used in "the branches reached out like spindly witches' fingers"?
   - A   Simile
   - B   Metaphor
   - C   Onomatopoeia
   - D   None of the above

3. What type of word is "wintry"? (line 1)
   - A   A verb
   - B   A noun
   - C   An adverb
   - D   An adjective

4. Who is Sidney in this passage? (line 15)
   - A   Her brother
   - B   Her dog
   - C   Her cat
   - D   Her rabbit

5. Which word class is "happiness"? (line 19)
   - A   A verb
   - B   An adjective
   - C   An abstract noun
   - D   An adverb

6. What word best describes the mood that has been set in the first paragraph?
   - A   Lighthearted
   - B   Tense
   - C   Easy
   - D   Petrifying

7. Where is Allegra walking in the second paragraph?
   - A   In her house
   - B   In the forest
   - C   To school
   - D   Along her street

(8) When was the story set?
- A August
- B March
- C April
- D November

(9) In the first paragraph, what made Allegra feel uncomfortable?
- A The particularly bad weather conditions
- B Her legs were tired
- C She wasn't used to walking in the woods
- D It was a spooky forest.

(10) Why did her mood change in the second paragraph?
- A She went into the forest.
- B She was home.
- C She saw her friend's house.
- D The weather got better.

(11) What does the author mean when she said things "worked like clockwork"? (line 20)
- A They had lots of clocks in the house.
- B They did everything at a certain time.
- C They needed their clocks to work all the time.
- D They didn't care at what time things happened.

(12) What did the wind sound like?
- A A flute
- B Pan pipes
- C Pitch pipes
- D Wind chimes

(13) What does the term "nit-picking" mean? (line 32)
- A Picking on small insignificant things
- B Picking on horrible things
- C Being very unpleasant
- D Not being very kind

(14) Which two words would best describe Allegra's mother?
- A Relaxed and free spirited
- B Uptight and a perfectionist
- C Laidback and fun-loving
- D Highly strung and irritable

(15) What does "spontaneous" mean? (line 21)
- [ ] **A** Carefully planned
- [ ] **B** Fiery
- [ ] **C** Without planning
- [ ] **D** Frightening

(16) How did Allegra know that her dinner would be on the table at 6:00pm?
- [ ] **A** Because there were toast crumbs on the table.
- [ ] **B** Because everything had a set time slot.
- [ ] **C** Dad was arriving at 5:30pm.
- [ ] **D** Because she had done her homework.

(17) Which two words would best summarise how Allegra feels in this passage?
- [ ] **A** Concerned then frustrated
- [ ] **B** Terrified then content
- [ ] **C** Scared then happy
- [ ] **D** Brave then elated

(18) What is a synonym for the word "wrath"? (line 29)
- [ ] **A** Fury
- [ ] **B** Crazy
- [ ] **C** Calm
- [ ] **D** Excited

(19) What is the word class of the word "extreme"? (line 5)
- [ ] **A** A verb
- [ ] **B** An adverb
- [ ] **C** A noun
- [ ] **D** An adjective

(20) Why does the author use the image of "spindly witches' fingers" in the opening paragraph?
- [ ] **A** The branches were grabbing the air.
- [ ] **B** It creates a sinister tone.
- [ ] **C** They looked like witches.
- [ ] **D** There is no reason for the imagery.

BILLY'S SMART SIMILES

The passage titled 'Forest' uses descriptive language to bring the story alive. In the opening paragraph, there is the line '*the whistling of the wind sounded like pitch pipes.*' This is an example of a simile. These are phrases which compare something to something else using 'like' or 'as'. The two things compared have similar characteristics. Can you help Billy complete these well-known similes?

1. Oliver is as cunning as a _____.

2. The soldier was as brave as a _____.

3. The well was as dry as a _____.

4. The teacher is as wise as an _____.

5. My friend sings like an _____.

6. When we are finished, the house is as clean as a _____.

7. My grandmother is as deaf as a _____.

8. After winning the chess tournament, he was as proud as a _____.

> **Similes may be confused with metaphors, which do the same kind of thing. Similes use comparisons with the words 'like' or 'as'.**
> **A metaphor is a figure of speech containing an implied comparison.**

17. PINOCCHIO

15:00
15 minutes

1 Little as Geppetto's house was, it was neat and comfortable. It was a small room on the ground floor, with a tiny window under the stairway. The furniture could not have been much simpler: a very old chair, a rickety old bed, and a tumble-down table. A fireplace full of burning logs was painted on the wall opposite the door. Over the fire, there was
5 painted a pot full of something which kept boiling happily away and sending up clouds of what looked like real steam.

As soon as he reached home, Geppetto took his tools and began to cut and shape the wood into a Marionette. "What shall I call him?" he said to himself. "I think I'll call him PINOCCHIO. This name will make his fortune. I knew a whole family of Pinocchi once
10 -- Pinocchio the father, Pinocchia the mother, and Pinocchi the children -- and they were all lucky. The richest of them begged for his living." After choosing the name for his Marionette, Geppetto set seriously to work to make the hair, the forehead, the eyes. Fancy his surprise when he noticed that these eyes moved and then stared fixedly at him. Geppetto, seeing this, felt insulted and said in a grieved tone: "Ugly wooden eyes, why
15 do you stare so?" There was no answer.

After the eyes, Geppetto made the nose, which began to stretch as soon as finished. It stretched and stretched and stretched till it became so long, it seemed endless. Poor Geppetto kept cutting it and cutting it, but the more he cut, the longer grew that impertinent nose. In despair he let it alone. Next he made the mouth. No sooner was
20 it finished than it began to laugh and poke fun at him. "Stop laughing!" said Geppetto angrily; but he might as well have spoken to the wall. "Stop laughing, I say!" he roared in a voice of thunder. The mouth stopped laughing, but it stuck out a long tongue.

Not wishing to start an argument, Geppetto made believe he saw nothing and went on with his work. After the mouth, he made the chin, then the neck, the shoulders,
25 the stomach, the arms, and the hands. As he was about to put the last touches on the finger tips, Geppetto felt his wig being pulled off. He glanced up and what did he see? His yellow wig was in the Marionette's hand. "Pinocchio, give me my wig!" But instead of giving it back, Pinocchio put it on his own head, which was half swallowed up in it. At that unexpected trick, Geppetto became very sad and downcast, more so than he had
30 ever been before. "Pinocchio, you wicked boy!" he cried out. "You are not yet finished, and you start out by being impudent to your poor old father. Very bad, my son, very bad!" And he wiped away a tear.

The legs and feet still had to be made. As soon as they were done, Geppetto felt a sharp kick on the tip of his nose. "I deserve it!" he said to himself. "I should have thought of this
35 before I made him. Now it's too late!" He took hold of the Marionette under the arms and put him on the floor to teach him to walk. Pinocchio's legs were so stiff that he could not move them, and Geppetto held his hand and showed him how to put out one foot after the other.

When his legs were limbered up, Pinocchio started walking by himself and ran all around
40   the room. He came to the open door, and with one leap he was out into the street.
Away he flew! Poor Geppetto ran after him but was unable to catch him, for Pinocchio
ran in leaps and bounds, his two wooden feet, as they beat on the stones of the street,
making as much noise as twenty peasants in wooden shoes. "Catch him! Catch him!"
Geppetto kept shouting. But the people in the street, seeing a wooden Marionette
45   running like the wind, stood still to stare and to laugh until they cried. At last, by sheer
luck, a Carabineer (or, military policeman) happened along, who, hearing all that noise,
thought that it might be a runaway colt, and stood bravely in the middle of the street,
with legs wide apart, firmly resolved to stop it and prevent any trouble. Pinocchio saw
the Carabineer from afar and tried his best to escape between the legs of the big fellow,
50   but without success. The Carabineer grabbed him by the nose (it was an extremely
long one and seemed made on purpose for that very thing) and returned him to Mastro
Geppetto.

17. PINOCCHIO questions

1. What literary device is used in this sentence from the text? '"Stop laughing, I say!" he roared in a voice of thunder.' (lines 21–22)
   - [ ] **A** Onomatopoeia
   - [ ] **B** Simile
   - [ ] **C** Metaphor
   - [ ] **D** Alliteration

2. Why did the author suggest that Geppetto "might as well have spoken to the wall"? (line 21)
   - [ ] **A** Pinocchio was not real.
   - [ ] **B** Pinocchio was not listening.
   - [ ] **C** Geppetto was mad.
   - [ ] **D** Because walls have ears.

3. What is a marionette? (line 8)
   - [ ] **A** A piece of wood
   - [ ] **B** A doll
   - [ ] **C** A puppet
   - [ ] **D** A boy

4. Why did Geppetto call him Pinocchio?
   - [ ] **A** He knew a family of Pinocchis, who were very lucky.
   - [ ] **B** He thought it was a nice name.
   - [ ] **C** Because his nose grew when he was dishonest.
   - [ ] **D** He had no reason.

5. What did Geppetto make first? (line 12)
   - [ ] **A** His body
   - [ ] **B** His legs
   - [ ] **C** His nose
   - [ ] **D** His hair

6. What is a synonym for "Impertinent"? (line 19)
   - [ ] **A** Disrespectful
   - [ ] **B** Determined
   - [ ] **C** Respectful
   - [ ] **D** Imperfect

7. What type of word is the word "unexpected" in this sentence from the text? "At that unexpected trick, Geppetto became very sad and downcast, more so than he had ever been before." (lines 28–30)
   - [ ] **A** An adverb
   - [ ] **B** An adjective
   - [ ] **C** A noun
   - [ ] **D** A verb

⑧ Why couldn't Pinocchio move his legs? (lines 36–37)

- ☐ **A** They were too flexible.
- ☐ **B** They were not complete.
- ☐ **C** He was not real.
- ☐ **D** They were too stiff.

⑨ What did the police officer think was coming down the street? (lines 46–47)

- ☐ **A** A criminal
- ☐ **B** Pinocchio
- ☐ **C** A horse
- ☐ **D** A man

⑩ What is the word class of the word "bravely"? (lines 45–48)

- ☐ **A** An adjective
- ☐ **B** An adverb
- ☐ **C** A noun
- ☐ **D** A verb

⑪ How does the author portray the character of Pinocchio?

- ☐ **A** Cheeky and mischievous
- ☐ **B** Well behaved and obedient
- ☐ **C** Inanimate and simple
- ☐ **D** Evil and manipulative

⑫ Why does the author use the words "Away he flew"? (line 41)

- ☐ **A** Pinocchio was flying.
- ☐ **B** He was a bird.
- ☐ **C** He was moving slowly and gracefully like a bird.
- ☐ **D** He was moving quickly.

⑬ What happened when Pinocchio stopped laughing? (line 22)

- ☐ **A** Geppetto stuck his tongue out at Pinocchio.
- ☐ **B** There was silence.
- ☐ **C** Pinocchio stuck his tongue out at Geppetto.
- ☐ **D** He started laughing again.

⑭ What type of literary device is the phrase "running like the wind"? (line 45)

- ☐ **A** Simile
- ☐ **B** Metaphor
- ☐ **C** Onomatopoeia
- ☐ **D** Sibilance

15. What made it easier to catch Pinocchio? (line 50)
- A   He wasn't running very fast.
- B   The policeman stood in the way.
- C   Pinocchio's nose was long.
- D   Pinocchio wasn't sneaky enough.

16. How do you think Geppetto was feeling about having made Pinocchio?
- A   Regretful
- B   Happy
- C   Indifferent
- D   Scared

17. Why were the people crying? (line 45)
- A   They were sad for Geppetto because Pinocchio was running away.
- B   They were crying with laughter.
- C   They were sad that Pinocchio wouldn't stop running.
- D   They were frustrated that nobody could catch him.

18. Why did Geppetto speak "in a grieved tone"? (line 14)
- A   He was insulted that Pinocchio was staring.
- B   He wanted a child of his own.
- C   He was annoyed that Pinocchio's eyes didn't look like he'd hoped.
- D   He was annoyed for no reason.

19. What did Pinocchio do with Geppetto's wig? (lines 27–28)
- A   He gave it back.
- B   He played with it.
- C   He put it on his own head.
- D   He threw it on the floor.

20. What did Geppetto have in his house? (lines 1–6)
- A   A fire and a rickety old bed
- B   A pot of something boiling and a very old chair
- C   A fire and a pot of something bubbling away
- D   A very old chair and a rickety old bed

BILLY'S SPLENDID SYNONYMS

The famous story of Pinocchio brings a puppet (Marionette) to life by using wonderful descriptive language. Having a wide vocabulary can help when using similar words. In the first paragraph, the synonyms 'small' and 'tiny' are used to describe the room and window. Can you think of three synonyms for the following adjectives?

Adjective	Synonym	Synonym	Synonym
old			
ugly			
poor			
sharp			
stiff			
wide			
big			
long			

It is useful to know synonyms so that you don't repeat words in your writing. One very simple game to play with a friend or family member is to record as many synonyms as possible for a certain word. For example, if you use the word 'quick', how many words can you think of that mean the same?

Quick _____ _____ _____ _____

_____ _____ _____ _____

Using a thesaurus can be a great way to learn synonyms and to enhance your word knowledge.

18. PLANETS

15:00
15 minutes

1   There are eight planets in our solar system: Mercury, Venus, Earth, Mars, Jupiter, Saturn,
Uranus and Neptune. These can be remembered with the mnemonic: 'My Very Educated
Mother Just Served Us Nachos'. They are ordered by their distance from the Sun. Planets
have to qualify in three main categories: they must orbit the Sun, have sufficient mass to
5   form a nearly round shape and have cleared the neighbourhood around their orbit.

The closest planet to the Sun, and the smallest, is Mercury. It also moves the fastest
around the Sun, which is where it gets its name from. The Roman God, Mercury used to
carry messages between the gods very quickly, thanks to his winged helmet and shoes.
Mercury is similar in appearance to the Moon and is covered in craters caused by falling
10 rocks. It has extremes of temperature; owing to its proximity to the Sun it gets very hot
but at night it becomes very cold because, unlike the Earth, it does not have a blanket
of air around it.

Venus is the second closest planet to the Sun and was named after the Roman goddess
of love and beauty, Venus. Venus is the second brightest object in the sky at night and is
15 even visible sometimes during the day. It appears to be a cloudy white colour because
of the opaque layer of clouds that covers its surface. Venus rotates in the opposite
direction to most other planets and it has been speculated that this could be due to an
impact from an asteroid many years ago that changed its rotational direction.

Mars is the second smallest planet in the solar system and is named after the Roman god
20 of war. It is sometimes called the 'Red Planet' because it appears red in colour. Olympus
Mons is the tallest mountain in the solar system and it can be found on Mars. Mars is a
more elongated shape than the other planets which causes extreme seasons owing to its
orbital path around the Sun.

Jupiter is one of the gas giant planets because it is largely made up of gases. It is by far
25 the largest planet in the solar system and has a storm that has been raging for hundreds
of years, known as the 'Red Spot'.

Saturn is the most distant planet that can be seen by the naked eye from Earth and is
the second largest planet. It is surrounded by a ring system that was first observed by
Galileo Galilei and is made of mainly hydrogen. It has 150 moons and smaller moonlets
30 and lakes of liquid methane as well as frozen nitrogen landscapes.

Uranus was not originally thought to be a planet because it orbits very slowly and was
very dim in the sky. It is also at an angle in comparison to the other planets because it
tilts on its axis. Like many other planets, Uranus is sometimes referred to by another
name – the 'Ice Giant.' It is pale blue in colour and this is caused by the water, ammonia
35 and methane ice crystals that form its upper atmosphere.

Neptune is the furthest planet away from the Sun and was named after the Roman god of the sea. It spins on its axis very quickly and it is not a solid body. The inner core of the planet is solid but there are also layers of liquids and gases. Neptune has a very active climate and had a storm called the 'Great Dark Spot' that lasted for around five years.

39

Non-fiction uses some vocabulary that is not found in stories.

18. PLANETS questions

1. Which planet is furthest from the Sun? (lines 1–3)
   - [ ] **A** Earth
   - [ ] **B** Uranus
   - [ ] **C** Venus
   - [ ] **D** Neptune

2. Which of the following is true of all planets? (lines 3–5)
   - [ ] **A** There is water.
   - [ ] **B** There is life.
   - [ ] **C** They orbit the Sun.
   - [ ] **D** A planet has all the above.

3. What is the purpose of the colon in line 4?
   - [ ] **A** To replace a comma
   - [ ] **B** To indicate the end of a sentence
   - [ ] **C** To introduce a list
   - [ ] **D** To replace a semi-colon

4. What does "orbit" mean?
   - [ ] **A** Moves in straight lines
   - [ ] **B** Moves quickly
   - [ ] **C** Spins on its axis
   - [ ] **D** Moves in a circle around something else

5. What does the word "sufficient" mean? (line 4)
   - [ ] **A** Too much
   - [ ] **B** Enough
   - [ ] **C** Too little
   - [ ] **D** An excess of

6. Why are mnemonics useful? (line 2)
   - [ ] **A** They are funny.
   - [ ] **B** They are related to what people are trying to learn
   - [ ] **C** They are very short.
   - [ ] **D** They are memorable.

7. Why haven't astronauts visited Mercury? (lines 9–12)
   - [ ] **A** They are not interested in the planet.
   - [ ] **B** It is uninhabitable.
   - [ ] **C** It is too close to the Sun.
   - [ ] **D** They already know everything about it.

8. Where does Mercury get its name from? (lines 7–8)

- [ ] **A** There is no logical reason.
- [ ] **B** From the messenger for the Roman gods
- [ ] **C** A Roman god
- [ ] **D** The element Mercury

9. What do you think is the brightest object in the sky at night?

- [ ] **A** The Sun
- [ ] **B** The Moon
- [ ] **C** The stars
- [ ] **D** Venus

10. What does the word "opaque" mean? (line 16)

- [ ] **A** Not transparent
- [ ] **B** Transparent
- [ ] **C** See-through
- [ ] **D** Reflective

11. Why does Venus have a different rotational direction to most planets? (lines 16–18)

- [ ] **A** It is unknown but scientists have come up with theories.
- [ ] **B** It has always rotated in the opposite direction.
- [ ] **C** It was caused by the impact of an asteroid.
- [ ] **D** It collided with another planet.

12. Why does Mars have extreme weather conditions? (lines 21–23)

- [ ] **A** Because of its mountain.
- [ ] **B** Because of its size.
- [ ] **C** Its shape causes its orbital path to take longer.
- [ ] **D** It is close to the Sun.

13. Neptune "is not a solid body" means:

- [ ] **A** Its inner core is hollow
- [ ] **B** Its outer layers are fluid
- [ ] **C** It is very fat
- [ ] **D** It has lots of storms

14. Who do you think Galileo Galilei was? (line 29)

- [ ] **A** An astronomer
- [ ] **B** An astronaut
- [ ] **C** A biologist
- [ ] **D** A doctor

(15) What causes Uranus to be a pale blue colour? (lines 34–35)

- [ ] **A** The water
- [ ] **B** The ammonia
- [ ] **C** The methane ice crystals
- [ ] **D** All of the above

(16) How long did the storm on Neptune last?

- [ ] **A** Exactly five years
- [ ] **B** Five days
- [ ] **C** Roughly five years
- [ ] **D** Around five months

(17) What is a synonym for "mainly"? (line 29)

- [ ] **A** Predominantly
- [ ] **B** Partially
- [ ] **C** Insignificantly
- [ ] **D** Incompletely

(18) Which is the smallest planet?

- [ ] **A** Earth
- [ ] **B** Mercury
- [ ] **C** Mars
- [ ] **D** Venus

(19) What colour is Venus?

- [ ] **A** White
- [ ] **B** Red
- [ ] **C** Blue
- [ ] **D** Orange

(20) Which planet is the furthest that can be seen by the naked eye? (line 27)

- [ ] **A** Saturn
- [ ] **B** Jupiter
- [ ] **C** Uranus
- [ ] **D** Neptune

BILLY'S MEMORABLE MNEMONICS

Mnemonics can be a useful system to remember ideas, associations or pattern of letters. Often, they can be comical, and they should help improve your memory. In the previous passage there is a mnemonic used to remember the order of the planets.

My **V**ery **E**ducated **M**other **J**ust **S**erved **U**s **N**achos

Below are some more well-known acronym mnemonics.

To help remember the colours of the rainbow:

ROY.G.BIV – **R**ed, **O**range, **Y**ellow, **G**reen, **B**lue, **I**ndigo and **V**iolet.

To help spell the word tomorrow:

TOMORROW – **T**rails **O**f **M**y **O**ld **R**ed **R**ose **O**ver **W**indow.

To help spell the word Geography:

GEOGRAPHY – **G**eorge's **E**lderly **O**ld **G**randfather **R**ode **A** **P**ig **H**ome **Y**esterday

A rhyme mnemonic to help remember the number of days in each month:

Thirty days hath September, April, June and November;

All the rest have thirty one.

Try and create your own mnemonics based in the items below.

Body excretory organs
Liver, kidney, Skin, Lungs, Intestines

_____

Shopping list
Bread, cucumber, eggs, lettuce, cream, tomatoes

_____

Properties of matter
Mass, weight, volume, density

_____

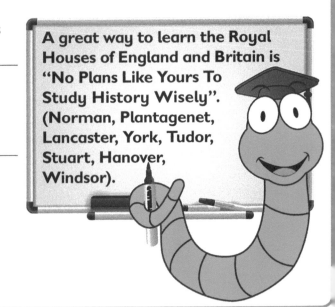

A great way to learn the Royal Houses of England and Britain is "No Plans Like Yours To Study History Wisely". (Norman, Plantagenet, Lancaster, York, Tudor, Stuart, Hanover, Windsor).

19. THE VELVETEEN RABBIT

15:00
15 minutes

1 THERE was once a velveteen rabbit, and in the beginning he was really splendid. He was fat and bunchy, as a rabbit should be; his coat was spotted brown and white, he had real thread whiskers, and his ears were lined with pink sateen. One Christmas morning, when he sat wedged in the top of the Boy's stocking, with a sprig of holly between his paws,
5 the effect was charming.

There were other things in the stocking, nuts and oranges and a toy engine, and chocolate almonds and a clockwork mouse, but the Rabbit was quite the best of all.

For at least two hours the Boy loved him, and then Aunts and Uncles came to dinner, and there was a great rustling of tissue paper and unwrapping of parcels, and in the
10 excitement of looking at all the new presents the Velveteen Rabbit was forgotten.

Christmas Morning

For a long time he lived in the toy cupboard or on the nursery floor, and no one thought very much about him. He was naturally shy and being only made of velveteen, some of the more expensive toys quite snubbed him. The mechanical toys were very superior,
15 and looked down upon everyone else; they were full of modern ideas, and pretended they were real. The model boat, who had lived through two seasons and lost most of his paint, caught the tone from them and never missed an opportunity of referring to his rigging in technical terms. The Rabbit could not claim to be a model of anything, for he didn't know that real rabbits existed; he thought they were all stuffed with sawdust
20 like himself, and he understood that sawdust was quite out-of-date and should never be mentioned in modern circles. Even Timothy, the jointed wooden lion, who was made by the disabled soldiers, and should have had broader views, put on airs and pretended he was connected with Government. Between them all the poor little Rabbit was made to feel himself very insignificant and commonplace, and the only person who was kind to
25 him at all was the Skin Horse.

The Skin Horse had lived longer in the nursery than any of the others. He was so old that his brown coat was bald in patches and showed the seams underneath, and most of the hairs in his tail had been pulled out to string bead necklaces. He was wise, for he had seen a long succession of mechanical toys arrive to boast and swagger, and by-the-by
30 break their mainspring and pass away, and he knew that they were only toys, and would never turn into anything else. For nursery magic is very strange and wonderful, and only those playthings that are old and wise and experienced like the Skin Horse understand all about it.

"What is REAL?" asked the Rabbit one day, when they were lying side by side near the
35 nursery fender, before Nana came to tidy the room. "Does it mean having things that buzz inside you and a stick-out handle?"

"Real isn't how you are made," said the Skin Horse. "It's a thing that happens to you. When a child loves you for a long, long time, not just to play with, but REALLY loves you, then you become Real."

40 "Does it hurt?" asked the Rabbit.

"Sometimes," said the Skin Horse, for he was always truthful. "When you are Real you don't mind being hurt."

"Does it happen all at once, like being wound up," he asked, "or bit by bit?"

"It doesn't happen all at once," said the Skin Horse. "You become. It takes a long time.
45 That's why it doesn't happen often to people who break easily, or have sharp edges, or who have to be carefully kept. Generally, by the time you are Real, most of your hair has been loved off, and your eyes drop out and you get loose in the joints and very shabby. But these things don't matter at all, because once you are Real you can't be ugly, except to people who don't understand."

50 "I suppose you are real?" said the Rabbit. And then he wished he had not said it, for he thought the Skin Horse might be sensitive. But the Skin Horse only smiled.

19. THE VELVETEEN RABBIT questions

① When was the story set?
- ☐ **A** January
- ☐ **B** August
- ☐ **C** June
- ☐ **D** December

② What did the Velveteen Rabbit want?
- ☐ **A** To be real
- ☐ **B** To feel important
- ☐ **C** To be played with
- ☐ **D** To see a real rabbit

③ Why did the Rabbit question the Skin Horse?
- ☐ **A** He was real.
- ☐ **B** He was old.
- ☐ **C** He was considered to be knowledgeable.
- ☐ **D** He was the only toy that the Velveteen Rabbit wanted to talk to.

④ Why did the Rabbit suppose the Skin Horse was real?
- ☐ **A** He was very old.
- ☐ **B** He was wise.
- ☐ **C** He looked like the toys he had described.
- ☐ **D** He knew a lot about being real.

⑤ What is the word class of the word "carefully"? (line 46)
- ☐ **A** An adjective
- ☐ **B** An adverb
- ☐ **C** A noun
- ☐ **D** A preposition

⑥ What was the Velveteen Rabbit afraid of?
- ☐ **A** Being in pain
- ☐ **B** Not being loved
- ☐ **C** Being real
- ☐ **D** Being abandoned

⑦ What is an antonym for "superior"? (line 14)
- ☐ **A** Greater
- ☐ **B** Smaller
- ☐ **C** Unimportant
- ☐ **D** Substandard

8. What does the word "snubbed" mean? (line 14)
   - [ ] **A** To be rude to someone
   - [ ] **B** To not give someone enough attention
   - [ ] **C** To insult someone
   - [ ] **D** To be kind and caring towards someone

9. Who made Timothy? (lines 21–22)
   - [ ] **A** Active soldiers
   - [ ] **B** Toy makers
   - [ ] **C** Disabled soldiers
   - [ ] **D** The text does not specify.

10. Why is "REALLY" in capital letters? (line 38)
    - [ ] **A** They are shouting.
    - [ ] **B** They are emphasising 'really'.
    - [ ] **C** It is a typo.
    - [ ] **D** It is a proper noun.

11. Why had the hairs in the horse's tail been removed? (lines 27–28)
    - [ ] **A** They were used to make bead necklaces.
    - [ ] **B** They had been pulled out when the children were playing with him.
    - [ ] **C** They fell out because he was old.
    - [ ] **D** The information is not in the text.

12. Which two words would best describe the character of the Velveteen Rabbit?
    - [ ] **A** Outgoing and extroverted
    - [ ] **B** Shy and insecure
    - [ ] **C** Introverted and depressed
    - [ ] **D** Nervous and anxious

13. Why do you think the boat had lost most of its paint? (lines 16–17)
    - [ ] **A** He was old and it had chipped off.
    - [ ] **B** He was not painted very well to begin with.
    - [ ] **C** He has been played with a lot.
    - [ ] **D** He has been in the sea.

14. Why was the Velveteen Rabbit forgotten? (lines 8–10)
    - [ ] **A** He was not that special.
    - [ ] **B** The boy unwrapped his new presents.
    - [ ] **C** The boy didn't like him very much.
    - [ ] **D** His uncles and aunties came to the house.

(15) What edible things were in the stocking with the Velveteen Rabbit? (lines 6–7)
- ☐ **A** A sprig of holly and a toy engine
- ☐ **B** A clockwork mouse and chocolate almonds
- ☐ **C** Nuts and oranges
- ☐ **D** A toy engine and a clockwork mouse

(16) According to the Skin Horse, why did a lot of the mechanical toys not become real? (lines 28–31)
- ☐ **A** They were not loved enough by the boy.
- ☐ **B** They were not magical enough.
- ☐ **C** They would break too easily.
- ☐ **D** They did not want to be real.

(17) What does the Rabbit think makes a toy real? (lines 34–36)
- ☐ **A** One which has a squeaker
- ☐ **B** One which can move
- ☐ **C** One which is soft and squidgy
- ☐ **D** One which has a buzz inside

(18) Who would be the "people who don't understand"? (line 49)
- ☐ **A** The people who don't love you
- ☐ **B** Grown up people
- ☐ **C** Other toys
- ☐ **D** Children

(19) What type of word is the word "excitement"? (line 10)
- ☐ **A** A verb
- ☐ **B** An abstract noun
- ☐ **C** A concrete noun
- ☐ **D** An adjective

(20) What colour was the Velveteen Rabbit? (line 2)
- ☐ **A** Brown
- ☐ **B** White
- ☐ **C** Grey
- ☐ **D** Brown and white

BILLY'S NUMEROUS NOUNS

In the last comprehension passage, the Rabbit is trying to understand 'What is real?'. The Velveteen Rabbit is a toy, which is a noun. This page explores the different types of nouns. Firstly, common nouns are naming words for people, places, animals and things. Proper nouns name things that begin with a capital letter. An abstract noun is something that you know exists but cannot take a photograph of, for example greed, love.

Below is a table containing different types of nouns. Can you place them under the correct headings?

joy	table	Rome	bravery	Joypreet	car
Berlin	love	clock	Thursday	metal	
fear	envy	Russia	bridge		

Common Nouns	Proper Nouns	Abstract nouns

There are other types of nouns. One other type is called 'collective nouns'. Collective nouns refer to groups of things, people or animals, e.g. class (of pupils). Can you add the animal group these collective nouns refer to?

1. pod _____
2. swarm _____
3. bunch _____
4. shrewdness _____
5. gaggle _____
6. troop _____

Pronouns can be used instead of nouns. They avoid using a name repeatedly. Examples include: 'I', 'you', 'he', 'she', 'it', 'we', 'they', 'me', 'him', 'her', 'us', and 'them'.

20. VOLCANOES

1 There are around 1510 active volcanoes in the world, and at any given time there are an average of 20 erupting at any one time. These eruptions act as giant safety valves to release the pressure that has built up inside the Earth. Volcanoes fall into three main categories: active, dormant or extinct. Active volcanoes are any that have erupted in the

5 past 1000 years and are likely to erupt again. Dormant volcanoes have not erupted in the past 1000 years but there is a chance that they might do so, and extinct volcanoes are unlikely to erupt again.

How volcanoes work

According to a theory, known as plate tectonics, the Earth's crust is broken into rigid

10 plates that form the surface of the planet. These plates are not static but move as a result of the pressure from the heat energy that comes from the centre of the planet. This pressure means that the plates move towards or away from each other and can also overlap. Volcanoes form near coastal areas where a land plate and an oceanic plate move towards each other. The oceanic plate is pushed down towards the centre of the

15 Earth which melts the rock and creates a hot magma that then rises towards the Earth's surface. When the magma reaches the crust, it collects in a reservoir until the pressure builds and then the magma is forced up through the Earth's crust.

How volcanoes erupt

There are four phases of volcanic eruption: Hawaiian, Strombolian, Vulcanian and

20 Peleean. In the Hawaiian phase, the lava is runny and gushes out rather than erupting. The second phase involves thicker lava and some mild explosions. In this phase there are also clouds of ash that drizzle the volcano with molten lava. The Vulcanian phase occurs if the magma plug has blocked the vent and, when the pressure builds, there is an explosive eruption and the magma is almost solid. The Peleean phase involves fine ash,

25 thick lava and gas-charged clouds which travel downhill at tremendous speeds.

Volcanic disaster

Volcanoes are among the most devastating and dangerous natural forces, both in the past and in the present. There have been many examples of when volcanoes have caused a tragic loss of life. A famous example, and the most catastrophic example in European

30 history, is when Mount Vesuvius buried the Roman city of Pompeii. The volcanic ash preserved the bodies of the residents until they were uncovered in 1748. When the bodies were uncovered, it portrayed what life would have been like on a typical morning in Pompeii in AD79.

Another more recent devastating eruption originated from Mount Tambora in Indonesia

35 between 1815 and 1816 and resulted in a death toll of more than 92,000 people. The volcano that originally stood at 13,000 feet was reduced to 9,000. The ash that gathered in the atmosphere as a result of this eruption reduced the temperature

worldwide and 1816 became known as 'the year without summer'. The death toll was much higher than the original 92,000 owing to the lack of summer and to crop failures

40 since crops as far away as Europe and America were affected.

Volcanic benefits

Although there are many examples of volcanic disasters, there are also many positives. The soil surrounding volcanoes is extremely fertile and is perfect for growing crops and plants. The heat from the magma is also used in areas such as Iceland to produce hot

45 water and run power plants. In Japan people bathe in warm volcanic sand because it is supposed to cure skin conditions and certain illnesses.

20. VOLCANOES questions

① What are extinct volcanoes?
- [ ] **A** Volcanoes that were around at the time of the dinosaurs.
- [ ] **B** Volcanoes that have erupted in the past 1000 years.
- [ ] **C** Volcanoes that are likely to erupt again.
- [ ] **D** Volcanoes that are unlikely to erupt again.

② What is a synonym for "preserved"? (line 31)
- [ ] **A** Maintained
- [ ] **B** Damaged
- [ ] **C** Used
- [ ] **D** Spoiled

③ Why has the author used the word "drizzle"? (line 22)
- [ ] **A** Because the rock is falling from the sky
- [ ] **B** Because it is raining when the volcanoes erupt
- [ ] **C** Because the lava is raining down lightly
- [ ] **D** Because the lava is falling heavily

④ Which phase of volcanic eruption involves thicker lava and mild explosions?
- [ ] **A** Hawaiian
- [ ] **B** Vulcanian
- [ ] **C** Strombolian
- [ ] **D** Peleean

⑤ In what year did Mount Vesuvius famously erupt in Pompeii?
- [ ] **A** 1748
- [ ] **B** AD79
- [ ] **C** 1784
- [ ] **D** AD76

⑥ Why would farmers choose to live by the volcanoes? (lines 43–44)
- [ ] **A** They like the warmth from the volcanoes.
- [ ] **B** They like to live in dangerous places.
- [ ] **C** The land around the volcanoes is very fertile.
- [ ] **D** They get sick a lot and need to bathe in the sand to make them better.

⑦ What causes the tectonic plates to move? (lines 10–11)
- [ ] **A** The Earth moving on its axis.
- [ ] **B** The ocean tides moving in and out.
- [ ] **C** They move by themselves.
- [ ] **D** The pressure from the Earth's core.

(8) What does a reservoir do? (line 16)
   A   Allows a liquid to move freely
   B   Stores a liquid
   C   Protects a liquid from pressure
   D   Allows a liquid to solidify

(9) What happens in the Peleean phase of volcanic eruption?
   A   There is fine ash, thick lava and gas charged clouds
   B   The magma plug blocks the vent
   C   The magma is almost solid
   D   The lava is thicker and there are mild explosions

(10) What is the magma most like in the Vulcanian phase?
   A   Gas
   B   Liquid
   C   Solid
   D   None of the above

(11) What is an antonym for "uncovered"? (line 31)
   A   Revealed
   B   Concealed
   C   Discovered
   D   Underground

(12) In what situation would there be a need for a safety valve? (line 2)
   A   To stop eruptions from happening
   B   To keep something flowing continuously
   C   To stop something from flowing continuously
   D   To release the pressure from something

(13) Why does the rock melt the closer it gets to the Earth's centre? (line 15)
   A   The centre of the Earth is cold.
   B   The centre of the Earth is the same temperature as the Earth's surface
   C   The centre of the Earth is hot.
   D   The plates melt easily.

(14) What is a synonym for "tragic"? (line 29)
   A   Fortunate
   B   Disastrous
   C   Lucky
   D   Sadness

15. Where does the magma originate? (lines 14–17)
- [ ] **A** From the eruption
- [ ] **B** From the sky
- [ ] **C** From the volcano
- [ ] **D** From the Earth's core

16. Where is Mount Vesuvius? (line 30)
- [ ] **A** America
- [ ] **B** Australia
- [ ] **C** Europe
- [ ] **D** Africa

17. What type of word is "produce" in this sentence from the text? 'The heat from the magma is also used in areas such as Iceland to produce hot water and run power plants.' (lines 44–45)
- [ ] **A** An adverb
- [ ] **B** A preposition
- [ ] **C** A verb
- [ ] **D** A noun

18. Why did the crops fail in 1816? (lines 36–40)
- [ ] **A** The lava destroyed the villages so they couldn't grow crops.
- [ ] **B** There was not enough rain to grow the crops.
- [ ] **C** The soil around the volcano was not ready for planting.
- [ ] **D** The ash in the atmosphere reduced the temperature.

19. Which two adjectives are in this sentence from the text? 'Volcanoes are among the most devastating and dangerous natural forces, both in the past and in the present.' (lines 27–28)
- [ ] **A** "volcanoes" and "forces"
- [ ] **B** "dangerous" and "among"
- [ ] **C** "present" and "forces"
- [ ] **D** "devastating" and "natural"

20. What does the word 'tremendous' imply in this sentence from the text? 'The Peleean phase involves fine ash, thick lava and gas-charged clouds which travel downhill at tremendous speeds.' (lines 24–25)
- [ ] **A** The lava was moving very quickly.
- [ ] **B** The lava was very dangerous.
- [ ] **C** The amount of lava was amazing.
- [ ] **D** It was scary to see all the lava coming down the hill.

BILLY'S POPULAR PREPOSITIONS

The non-fiction text on volcanoes uses prepositions to help describe the location of something in relation to something else. Can you identify the prepositions in the following line taken directly from the text?

'Volcanoes form near coastal areas when a land plate and an oceanic plate move towards each other'.

Did you find them? One is 'near' the other is 'towards'.

In the sentences below <u>underline</u> the preposition.

1. **The book was placed on the shelf.**

2. **The golden eagle soared above the clouds.**

3. **It is a large crate for milk.**

4. **He put the blue tiles on the wrong wall.**

5. **"I'll meet you at 6:30pm."**

Some prepositions are made up of more than one word. For example, 'They live here <u>because of</u> the local school'.

SECTION 2:
ANSWERS

Answers

1. Alice in Wonderland: questions (pages 11–14)

Question	Answer	Explanation
1.	B	The Duchess says "Here! You may nurse it a bit if you like. I must go and get ready to play croquet with the Queen."
2.	A	"Snorting" is onomatopoeia; "like a steam engine" is a simile.
3.	C	Alice felt it would be "quite absurd" to carry it further because it was so obviously a pig.
4.	E	"They're sure to kill it in a day or two wouldn't it be murder to leave it behind?" This shows Alice felt she would be held responsible for the baby's death if she didn't take it away.
5.	A	The baby held its arm and legs out in all directions just like a stafish.
6.	D	Throwing means the same as "flinging".
7.	E	The text doesn't say.
8.	C	The baby was "neither more nor less than a pig" means it had become a pig.
9.	A	Alice is the subject, while "the thing" is the object.
10.	D	Alice wondered if the baby was crying like a human baby. Evidence of tears would have shown her that it was.
11.	B	Humerous (1) and Fantasy (4)
12.	B	She thought that the baby was now a handsome pig rather than an ugly baby.
13.	D	The cat was on a bough which is a synonym for branch.
14.	E	Alice wasn't sure the cat would appreciate being called "Cheshire Puss".
15.	B	handsome means good looking
16.	D	Alice said, "Would you tell me, please, which way I ought to go from here?"
17.	C	Dissatisfied is the best antonym for the word "pleased".
18.	D	Alice has left the house when she brings the baby into the "open air", and she saw the pig "trot away quietly into the wood".
19.	C	Third person narrative - the pronoun "she" is used.
20.	A	This text was originally intended for children.

Alice in Wonderland – Perfect Pronouns (page 15)

1) I
2) you
3) She
4) yourself
5) herself
6) her

Answers

2. Dragons: questions (pages 18–21)

Question	Answer	Explanation
1.	B	The test says that Chinese dragons are "revered". Revered means respected.
2.	C	The author uses a rhetorical question to begin the text. It requires no answer and thus implies that she believes that everyone does like dragon stories.
3.	C	The sentence compares "she" with a dragon, therefore it is a metaphor.
4.	D	This proverb infers that a child's place is to be quiet and well behaved.
5.	C	The author is saying something that she does not believe to be true in an attempt to be humorous. This is an example of irony.
6.	E	The text says that European dragons have the ability to spew fire (3). It states that they have only animal intelligence but that Chinese dragons are very intelligent (4).
7.	A	The word "envisage" means to form a mental picture of something. This is a synonym for imagines.
8.	C	It is an adverb meaning "the opposite" or "on the other hand".
9.	D	The text states that his most disturbing feature "apart from his greed" is arrogance. "Apart from" means "except for", therefore the answer is greed.
10.	C	The text states that his "soft underbelly" is vulnerable. Vulnerable means "exposed to the possibility of attack" and underbelly is the stomach. His underbelly is described as "soft" so it wouldn't be well protected.
11.	A	The author has just portrayed Smaug very negatively, therefore we can assume this to be the basis of her surprise.
12.	E	The author says that Kent makes his point "powerfully". We can infer from this that she would consider him to be clever.
13.	B	The text says that 'Dungeons and Dragons' makes "heavy use" of dragons. This would mean that it uses them often or repeatedly.
14.	D	The pupil asserts that the teacher is a dragon "today", which suggest that she is not always strict. She shows humour in the passage. She is not always kind if she can be a dragon.
15.	E	Refer to line 2 where children are "simultaneously frightened and delighted". "Simultaneously" means at the same time. Terrified is a synonym for "frightened" and amazing and pleasurable are synonyms for delighted.
16.	C	"Malevolent" means wishing bad or evil to others. The opposite is benevolent, meaning wishing to do good.
17.	D	The test refers to the "supremacy" of the dragon. "Supremacy" means being superior to all others.

Answers

18.	A	The text refers to the "brave and the avaricious". "Avaricious" means greedy.
19.	C	The story is a moral tale from which most readers would benefit.
20.	B	The author says "I am neither familiar with nor interested in them". This implies indifference.

Dragons – Amazing Adjectives (page 22)

mythical giant, reptilian, winged, enormous, awesome, large, wingless, malevolent, super natural, intelligent, mighty, powerful, violent, cruel, intelligent, arrogant, reddish-gold, impervious, soft, vulnerable, complex, cute, little, tyrannical, loveable, defenceless, red, silver

Answers

3. Weathers: questions (pages 24–27)

Question	Answer	Explanation
1.	B	Blossom is on the chestnut tree, cuckoos have arrived and girls in summer dresses.
2.	A	"Showers betumble the chestnut spikes". These are the flowers of the chestnut tree – often known as 'candles' – which the rain has knocked off the tree.
3.	B	"Nestling" is an old word for chick/baby bird.
4.	E	Brown, bills, best.
5.	D	"The Traveller's Rest" is the name of the pub where people can sit outside in good weather.
6.	B	As the poet refers to himself – "And so do I" – it is written in the first person. The verbs are present tense – "This is" and "they sit".
7.	C	Girls "sprig-muslin drest". Muslin is a fabric and sprigs are flowery twigs which form the pattern on the fabric.
8.	A	Citizens are inhabitants of a country.
9.	B	The south and west are where most summer holiday destinations are.
10.	D	Dressed
11.	C	Avoids
12.	C	"Bills" come from the verb "to bill" which means singing of a bird.
13.	D	Beeches (= trees) drip in browns and duns (dull dark colours)
14.	A	The repetition of "and" enhances rhythm (1) and builds on the poet's picture of all the things which happen (3).
15.	A	"Drops on gate bars hang in a row"
16.	C	"Meadow rivulets (small rivers) overflow".
17.	D	"Rooks" is a common noun because it names a variety of bird, not one specific bird and therefore does not require a capital letter.
18.	E	"Rooks in families homeward go, And so do I."
19.	C	He likes it when "showers betumble the chestnut spikes" but "shuns" beeches dripping in browns and duns.
20.	A	The answer is "mild" as line 3 refers to "showers" and a shower is a brief and gentle rain. Also, in line 5 the birds are happy to sing, and line 7 refers to "maids come forth sprig-muslin drest".

Weathers – Robust Rhymes (page 28)

1) Likes, spikes   2) I, fly   3) Drest, west   4) Shuns, duns

5) I, ply   6) Throe, row   7) Row, go

Answers

4. The Merchant of Venice: questions (pages 30–32)

Question	Answer	Explanation
1.	C	"as" means "like". A simile compares two things using one of these words.
2.	C	An abstract noun identifies a concept or an idea that is not visible or concrete.
3.	A	"'Tis" is a contraction for "it is". "It" is a pronoun and "is" is third person singular present tense of the verb "to be".
4.	A	"Strict" and "stern" both mean to demand that rules are observed.
5.	E	"Strained" is a synonym for "forced". Portia means that no-one is compelled to show mercy, it just happens.
6.	E	The pronoun "it" refers to the noun "mercy".
7.	A	The word "becomes" in line 5 in this context means "to suit someone". So mercy suits the monarch (king) better than his crown.
8.	A	The word "shows" in line 7 means symbolises or demonstrates. The "dread and fear" people have is of the king's authority.
9.	A	In line 11 "it" refers to mercy which is "enthroned" in a king's heart. Enthroned in this context means "installed" or "put in".
10.	C	In line 12 "it" is an attribute to God. An attribute is a characteristic. "It" refers to mercy and mercy means compassionate. Therefore, God is compassionate.
11.	E	"show likest" in line 13 means "seems most alike" and the word "season" in this context means mix or add in the way that you season your food with salt and pepper.
12.	D	In line 17 Portia says "we do pray for mercy".
13.	C	Portia speaks of praying for forgiveness and says that if we do this, it suggests that we should give to others what we ask for ourselves.
14.	C	Portia wants to save Antonio. If she makes Shylock feel ashamed, then he will not wish to harm Antonio.
15.	C	Portia says "thy plea, which if thou follow". "Thy" means "your", "thou" means "you". So, if Shylock insists on his plea to take the flesh, the court "must give sentence" and allow it.
16.	D	"Tarry a little" (line 25) means "wait a moment".
17.	C	Portia says that he will be in trouble if he sheds "one drop of Christian blood" therefore he cannot shed any blood at all when taking the pound of flesh.
18.	E	Portia is clever. She disguises herself well. She finds a loophole in the wording of the law. "There is something else".
19.	C	"Confiscate" means to take away from.

Answers

20.	D	Shylock says "I crave the law" which means he strongly desires it. Then he asks the question "Is that the law?" He is likely to be very angry that he cannot do what he wishes.

The Merchant of Venice – Synonymous Shakespeare (page 33)

1) blesseth
2) mightiest
3) wherein doth sit
4) render
5) thou
6) follow
7) deeds
8) carryeth out
9) tarry a little
10) thy

Answers

5. Treasure Island: questions (pages 36–39)

Question	Answer	Explanation
1.	C	Jim's eyes "turned instinctively in the direction of the rattling gravel."
2.	D	"Spurt" is a synoynm of "spout".
3.	E	The figure moves with "great rapidity" which means very quickly. He hides behind a tree not a bush.
4.	C	Jim is brought to a "stand" by "terror" which means great fear. The "apparition" refers to the "creature".
5.	B	Lurking and skulking are synonyms meaning to hide with a sinister or cowardly motive.
6.	D	In this context, "manlike" is an adverb, describing how the man was running.
7.	B	Jim says he preferred the dangers he knew to those he didn't (line 7) so, as he didn't know the "creature", he was more frightened of it than Silver.
8.	A	A simile is a way of describing something by comparing it to something else.
9.	C	Jim began to recall what he had heard of cannibals so he is afraid that the man might eat him.
10.	D	Jim recollects (remembers) that he has a pistol. We can presume that he would use it to shoot any adversary.
11.	A	The author speaks of "courage" (bravery) in Jim's heart and his face "resolutely" (determinedly) set.
12.	E	The author uses the word "hesitated" which infers the man was undecided. We can assume that this is due to fear.
13.	D	Ben asserts that he hasn't spoken in a long time. We can assume that this is why his voice is "rusty".
14.	E	"Fancied" can be a synonym for something imagined or invented in the mind.
15.	C	Jim shows sympathy towards Ben in promising to give him the cheese he longs for if it is ever possible.
16.	B	Ben says he has been "marooned" which means "left behind" or "abandoned". This is a good definition for abandoned.
17.	C	The passage says that Ben holds his hands "in supplication" and this means to beg earnestly or humbly.
18.	A	The text says that Ben shows "a childish pleasure in the presence of a fellow creature" (3). We can assume that he is checking that Jim is real because he hasn't seen anyone for "three years" (4).
19.	C	The phrase "by the" in this context means "weighed by the"; a stone is an old measure of heavy weight.

20.	A	He has lived on goats (line 45). He does not express an opinion about what he has eaten and he asks for cheese but not specifically goat's cheese.

Treasure Island – Awesome Adverbs (page 40)

Some possible answers are given. Written in brackets are the actual adverbs used in the passage.

1) I set my face <u>decisively</u> (resolutely) for this man of the island and walked briskly towards him.

2) But he must have been watching me <u>carefully</u> (closely).

3) <u>Immediately</u> (instantly) the figure reappeared, and making a wide circuit, began to head me off.

4) And <u>instantaneously</u> (immediately) I began to prefer the dangers that I knew to those I knew not.

5) I turned on my heel, and looking <u>suddenly</u> (sharply) behind me over my shoulder, began to retrace my steps in the direction of the boats.

Answers

6. Anne of Green Gables: questions (pages 43–46)

Question	Answer	Explanation
1.	D	Marilla was expecting to see a boy as in line 4 the text states "Matthew Cuthbert, who's that?" she ejaculated. "Where is the boy?". She was amazed that a girl had arrived.
2.	B	The child's dress is described as ugly, not her.
3.	C	The child's eyes are eager and luminous so the best synonym is "bright".
4.	E	Matthew says "She couldn't be left there."
5.	E	"Animation" is a noun.
6.	A	"Suddenly she seemed to grasp the meaning of what had been said" that is, Matthew and Marilla wanted a boy.
7.	B	The best definition of "deprecatingly" is "disapprovingly".
8.	C	Although some of the other things are true, she began to cry because at that moment she realised she wasn't wanted.
9.	A	Marilla's expression is "a reluctant smile, rather rusty from long disuse".
10.	D	Marilla says "Well don't cry any more. We're not going to turn you out-of-doors tonight".
11.	C	Anne, (see line 39)
12.	D	She says "Cordelia is a perfectly elegant name." "Elegant" means stylish and graceful.
13.	D	We can see from the discussion that while Anne enjoys make-believe ("I've always imagined that my name was Cordelia", (Marilla is down-to-earth ("Anne is a real good plain sensible name" (3)
14.	B	"Fiddlesticks" is an old-fashioned exclamation meaning nonsense.
15.	E	In this context, "late years" are years that have recently passed.
16.	D	Anne says her name spelt with an E is "more distinguished". "Distinguished" means distinctive and worthy of respect.
17.	A	"Abundance" means a very large quantity of something.
18.	C	Anne has given the road and a lake these names on the way from the station.
19.	C	Third person narrative
20.	B	We can see Anne's and Marilla's temperaments are really different but that she has already made Marilla smile (3). It is likely, for the sake of the story, that she will be allowed to stay with Matthew and Marilla (2).

Anne of Green Gables – Rigorous Reporting clauses (page 47)

1) she ejaculated   2) she cried   3) she said eagerly
4) explained Anne   5) said the unsympathetic Marilla
6) asked Marilla

Answers

7. Oliver Twist: questions (pages 50–53)

Question	Answer	Explanation
1.	A	The word "taunt" means to intentionally annoy and upset someone to force them into a reaction. The best option is "jeers".
2.	B	The text says that Noah is "under the impression" that Oliver is going to cry. He then "returned to the charge," which means continued with his behaviour. We can infer from this that he wants to make Oliver cry, so the closest option is B.
3.	C	Oliver "knows" how it feels which infers that he has had a similar experience.
4.	D	The text says that this act, or event, "produced a material change in all his future prospects and proceedings" (line 3). A material change means that circumstances change, therefore D is the correct answer.
5.	A	Oliver says "Not YOU. . .". He does not want Noah to know that he has the power to upset him.
6.	A	"Immediate" describes the noun "precursor", therefore it is an adjective.
7.	B	The text describes Noah as malicious which means spiteful. He has no regard for Oliver's feelings and continues to be horrible to him.
8.	E	The text says that Mrs Sowerberry waited until "she was quite certain that it was consistent with the preservation of human life" – she wanted to be sure that her life would be safe.
9.	D	Noah "blubbered" which means he cried (1). He also calls out for "Charlotte!" and "Missis" which refers to Mrs Sowerberry (3).
10.	D	He is too stupid to understand the threat. Noah does not understand that Oliver's silence is an indication of mounting anger.
11.	A	In line 44 Noah says that "hung is more likely" than the other two options. More likely means "most probable" and hanging would be a death sentence.
12.	B	In line 48 it says that "the boy" – which refers to Oliver, was a "quiet child, mild dejected creature". This infers that he would not normally be aggressive. We cannot say that he would never be violent as he has just been so, but we can conclude that is a rare happening.
13.	B	In lines 48–49 it says that "harsh" means he had been badly treated, or bullied, in the past.
14.	C	The text tells us that Oliver and Noah "descended" into the kitchen. Descend means to move downwards, therefore the boys must have been upstairs.

15.	B	"Innocent" can mean harmless or innocuous. Noah intends to gain amusement but is too simple-minded to predict how deeply he will upset Oliver and consequently cannot predict the violence of his reaction. Later in the text the narrator refers to Noah's "small wits" suggesting that he is unintelligent.
16.	C	"Sobbing" is closest in meaning to snivelling
17.	A	Sarcasm is the use of words that are usually intended to mock or show contempt.
18.	D	To sneer means to look contemptuous. As Noah's last remark shows contempt for Oliver's mother, we can conclude from the author's description of Noah's face that he is sneering.
19.	E	Oliver's first aggressive action is to overturn the table.
20.	E	Oliver is clearly becoming angry as he speaks "sharply". The words are threatening, therefore E is the best answer.

Oliver Twist – Clever Commas (page 54)

Intent upon this innocent amusement, Noah put his feet on the table-cloth; and pulled Oliver's hair; and twitched his ears; and expressed his opinion that he was a 'sneak'; and furthermore announced his intention of coming to see him hanged, whenever that desirable event should take place; and entered upon various topics of petty annoyance, like a malicious and ill-conditioned charity-boy as he was. But, none of these taunts producing the desired effect of making Oliver cry, Noah attempted to be more facetious still; and in his attempt, did what many small wits, with far greater reputations than Noah, sometimes do to this day, when they want to be funny. He got rather personal.

Answers

8. Coming to America: questions (pages 57–60)

Question	Answer	Explanation
1.	C	"In 1492 Columbus sailed the ocean blue." (line 2)
2.	D	There is no mention in the text of tepees.
3.	A	Archaeologists have found the remains of a Viking settlement. (line 12)
4.	C	The word "chanted" is a past test form of the verb "chant", which means to say or shout repeatedly in a sing-song tone.
5.	D	He wanted to find a trade route to Asia.
6.	B	America is west across the Atlantic from Europe and the text says that Columbus was planning to sail "in a westerly direction".
7.	C	It is an adjective describing the "trading lands".
8.	D	Columbus thought he had reached India.
9.	B	The Mayflower
10.	A	They sought religious freedom.
11.	B	High status is closest in meaning to "prestigious".
12.	C	A harvest festival. (line 33)
13.	E	Safe is the opposite of "hazardous".
14.	B	In New York Harbour (or Harbor)
15.	D	There is no mention in the text of improving their education while the other factors are mentioned on lines 45–46.
16.	C	Airports
17.	D	The New World (2) and The Land of Opportunity (4)
18.	E	Pre-Columbian means before Columbus. He sailed to America in 1492.
19.	E	Holidaymakers are not mentioned
20.	D	Informative text

Coming to America – Exciting Emotions (page 61)

Example descriptive paragraph (using all 12 words)

The top of the trees could just be made out on the horizon. Christopher and his crew were elated and overjoyed at the sight of dry land. They stared at the land beyond, overwhelmed and thrilled by the rolling hills, embracing each other in exhausted huddles. This discovery brought exuberant celebrations and euphoric cheers. After the realisation of their find had finally dawned, they became suspicious and sceptical of the landscape, unsure of their destiny. The were satisfied and somewhat privileged, yet astonished at what could possibly be beyond the vast waters which they had come to know.

Answers

9. You are old, Father William: questions (pages 63–66)

Question	Answer	Explanation
1.	B	The young man asks why Father William incessantly stands on his head (1) and observes that he turned a back-somersault at the door (3).
2.	C	The boy observes that Father William is old (line 9) and fat (line 10) but in spite of this has the ability to do a somersault.
3.	E	In line 7, Father William states that he doesn't have brain: "I have none," so there is no brain to injure.
4.	B	The youth says that he "would hardly suppose" which means "doesn't think" that Father William's eye would be steady (able to focus).
5.	C	Father William offers to sell the ointment directly after he has explained that it kept him supple. We can infer that he was selling it to the boy for the same reason.
6.	D	In lines 22 and 23 Father William says that the strength of his jaw was the result of arguing legal cases with his wife.
7.	C	Goose bones and beaks are tough and hard. The youth thinks that Father William's jaws are too weak to eat anything tougher than suet.
8.	E	Father William says "that is enough" so we can deduce that he is tired of doing so.
9.	D	The question infers that the youth has the opposite view, therefore he is being critical. It would be insensitive to do this to an elder.
10.	C	The youth asks a lot of questions which means he is "inquisitive".
11.	B	"Constantly" is a synonym for "incessantly".
12.	A	This is an idiom which means pretending to be superior.
13.	B	The word "supple" means flexible.
14.	B	A "sage" is someone who is wise and therefore able to answer questions.
15.	A	The youth says that Father William has grown fat, therefore we can infer that he has grown fat in later life.
16.	B	"Perfectly" is an adverb as it modifies the verb "sure".
17.	A	"Pray" in this context is an archaic word used as a polite preface to a request.
18.	C	A couple means two and the cost is one shilling per box.

Answers

19.	E	In this context, "argue" means he practised his skills as a lawyer with his wife.
20.	B	In line 11, we are told that he "turned a back-somersault in at the door."

"You are old, Father William" – Special Speech Marks (page 67)

"You are old, Father William," the young man said,
"And your hair has become very white;
And yet you incessantly stand on your head –
Do you think, at your age, it is right?"

Name of the punctuation mark	Symbol
semi-colon	;
hyphen	-
exclamation mark	!
question mark	?
comma	,
apostrophe	'
colon	:

Answers

10. A Midsummer Night's Dream: questions (pages 69–72)

Question	Answer	Explanation
1.	A	"Wither wander thee?" means "where are you going?"
2.	B	The fairy wanders "over hill over dale", which is hills and valleys (1); "thorough flood, thorough fire", which is water and fires (3).
3.	E	"Swifter than the moon's sphere" The Fairy flies more quickly than the moon.
4.	C	Deliberate repetition (1), rhyme (2), alliteration (3).
5.	D	The best explanation is that she is putting dew (sprinkling water) on orbs (circles i.e. fairy rings on the grass).
6.	D	"The cowslips tall her pensioners be; In their gold coats spots you can see" Cowslips are meadow flowers.
7.	C	"Seek" means to look for and so the best antonym is "hide".
8.	B	In line 13, the fairy says she is going to look for dew drops and hang them in the cowslips' ears. She uses the metaphor "pearl" for the dew drop.
9.	C	"Our Queen and all her elves come here anon". The elves are the Queen's servants and "anon" means soon.
10.	B	Shakespeare sets out to attribute natural events to fairy (magical) activity, e.g. Putting dew on the grass That spotted flowers are really fairy rubies That flowers are fairy servants Thus the best answer is that nature is magical. He also describes natural phenomena, e.g. the moon orbiting the earth, alongside descriptions of fairy activity and further attributing natural events (e.g. dew forming on the grass) to fairy activity.
11.	C	Revels are a sort of entertainment.
12.	B	Oberon is in a cruel and angry mood. "Wrath" means anger.
13.	C	A child stolen from an Indian king. "A lovely boy, stolen from an Indian king." (line 32)
14.	B	Hath = has = present tense of the verb to have
15.	B	A changeling is a child who has been stolen from its cradle by fairies and replaced with a fairy baby.
16.	C	In lines 24 and 25 Puck says Oberon wants the child to "trace"(map) "the forest wild" (uncharted forest)
17.	A	By force or forcibly
18.	E	Alliteration
19.	C	"All their elves for fear creep into acorn cups". (line 31)
20.	C	The King and Queen will meet unexpectedly that night. "The King doth keep his revels here tonight; Take heed the Queen come not within his sight." (lines 18-19)

Answers

A Midsummer Night's Dream – Shakespeare's Synonyms (page 73)

Shakespearian word	Definition
brier	tangled mass of prickly plants
anon	soon; shortly
wrath	extreme anger
hath	has
whither	to what place or state
doth	does
changeling	an ugly, stupid or strange child left by fairies in a place of a pretty, charming child
spangled	cover with small sparkling objects

Answers

11. Journey to the Centre of the Earth: questions (pages 76–78)

Question	Answer	Explanation
1.	C	He was desperate to see what was on the paper.
2.	B	"Annoyed" is the closest in meaning to indignant, which means to be angry about something that you think is wrong or unfair.
3.	A	The professor explained that "it is a true and correct account of the Norwegian princess who reigned in Iceland". (line 15)
4.	C	"He received me into his study; a perfect museum." (line 1)
5.	C	This is a simile as it is introduced by the word "like".
6.	A	"I hoped at all events it was translated into German." (lines 15–16)
7.	D	The professor taught his nephew about the stories he was reading and the boy had catalogued the contents of his office.
8.	D	There are several parts in the text which suggest their relationship was formal such as he has "summoned me to his presence".
9.	C	Several parts of the text indicate how engaged and excited the professor was by the book such as "absorbed in a book", "Wonderful - wonderful!" and 'My uncle, however, was in raptures.'
10.	B	The passage is written in the first person because the character is writing from his perspective and uses words such as "I" and "me". It is fiction because it is not true/it is a story.
11.	C	Line 9 says that "He admired its binding." "Admired" is a synonym for "like".
12.	D	"Uncaring" is an antonym for "fond" which means to care about.
13.	A	He tapped his head: "Wonderful!" he cried, tapping his forehead."
14.	C	It means that the book was very old because the pages of books turn yellow with age.
15.	B	The text implies that the boy didn't want to seem impolite. He has already stated he is not interested and there is no reference to him wanting to know more or being uneducated. He has respect for the professor but is not afraid because he is able to ask questions and joke with him.
16.	C	The professor was frustrated as shown by the words "cried my uncle, angry at my ignorance".

17.	D	He valued the language it was written in: "His delight was to have found the original work in the Icelandic tongue, which he declared to be one of the most magnificent and yet simple idioms in the world."
18.	A	The professor was intelligent and educated because he had a large collection of books and could read them in different languages.
19.	B	He did not feel it was an appropriate time to tell a joke because his uncle, the professor, was serious about what he was reading and therefore a joke would have been out of place in that situation.
20.	D	"Translated" is a verb, written here in the past tense.

Incredible Idioms (page 79)

1.	arm; To be extremely expensive.
2.	leg; To wish a performer 'good luck'.
3.	cake; Something that is simple.
4.	two; When two people are involved.
5.	air; When something still needs to be resolved.
6.	stone; To achieve two objectives in one go.
7.	thumb; A rough principle or guide.
8.	steam; To release excess energy or emotion.

12. A New Start: questions (pages 82–84)

Question	Answer	Explanation
1.	B	The moral of the poem is summed up by the last two lines: "So if you're ever afraid to try something new, Give it a go – you may discover a new you."
2.	D	"Misinterpret" means that you don't understand something and is the opposite to "fathom" where you understand something.
3.	B	She feels sympathetic towards the mouse and this answer can be justified through her use of phrases such as "the cute little mouse".
4.	A	"an inkling" means a slight knowledge or suspicion about something.
5.	B	"And when people discovered him, he was met with some frowns. The frowns were accompanied by screams and some shrieks, And it took ladies some time to recover, some weeks."
6.	C	Stanza 6 is when he has reached the countryside and is feeling happier.
7.	C	He wanted to be happier: "He had a good feeling about his new start in life, He had an inkling he'd live with minimum strife."

Answers

8.	C	'The cute little mouse couldn't fathom out why, Just his appearance would make people cry, And that is the reason he chose to be sneaky, He crawled through dark sewage pipes that were often quite leaky. It was a horrible life to keep sneaking around, Hoping that he would never be found.'
9.	D	'So our little mouse followed the mouse conga train' shows that the main mouse in the story is at the back of the line.
10.	B	"Tickled" describes what the blades of grass are doing and is therefore a verb.
11.	A	"Deliberated" means the same as thinking and pondering.
12.	B	The mouse is not a threat to anyone and, because he scares people, he hides away more. He is also described as cute and little.
13.	C	"He had lived in the city, since he was very small."
14.	A	All the sounds that are described within the stanza are relaxing and peaceful. The mouse also sighs and this creates a tranquil mood.
15.	C	These two lines tell you that the music made the mouse feel happy and upbeat: "His iPod was playing all his favourite songs. It helped him to feel somewhat upbeat" (lines 34–35)
16.	B	"And when peo-ple dis-cov-ered him, he was met with some frowns." There are 14 syllables.
17.	A	"Conflict" means disagreement or problems which is a synonym for "strife".
18.	C	"Unsnarl" means to untangle something.
19.	C	"And surrounding the flowers he heard the buzzing of bees."
20.	A	"Content" is a state of being happy and this describes how the mouse feels at the end of the poem, for example: "How wonderful it is to find somewhere new and so nice".

Perfect Personification (page 85) (Example answers:)

Sport	The ball took on a mind of its own and eventually found its way into the back of the net.
Animals	The leashed dog cried for his freedom.
Weather	The dark clouds had been threatening rain all day.
Vehicles	Trucks snarled through the heavy city traffic.

Answers

13: Ants: questions (pages 88–90)

Question	Answer	Explanation
1.	B	"Metamorphosis" means a change in the form, and often the habits, of an animal during normal development after the embryonic stage.
2.	C	"Ants are very social animals and they live in colonies." (line 7)
3.	A	"Ants are insects with six legs and bodies that are divided into three main parts: the head, thorax and abdomen." (line 1)
4.	D	The text says there are "as many as 10,000 trillion ants alive at any one time, in the world". (line 4)
5.	A	"During the winter months the ants will use the chambers further down in the nest where it is less frosty." (line 14)
6.	D	"She is the largest ant and has a larger abdomen than the other ants because she lays all the eggs." (line 22)
7.	C	"Male ants are generally smaller than the queen and their task is to fly away and mate with other queens." (lines 28 and 29)
8.	C	"A colony of wood ants can gather up to 100,000 caterpillars in just one day."
9.	B	"Some ants even build tunnels to allow air to enter and leave the nest, which act as an air conditioning system."
10.	C	In this context it does not mean "friend" but instead "reproduce": "Male ants are generally smaller than the queen and their task is to fly away and mate with other queens."
11.	A	"The majority of ants in a colony are worker ants and they are all wingless and female. Unlike most other animals the female workers do not reproduce but rather they gather food, build the nest, care for the eggs and feed the queen ant."
12.	C	"Ant eaters have special sticky tongues that allow them to eat several ants at a time."
13.	A	"Innumerable" means many. Other synonyms include countless, uncountable and a myriad.
14.	B	Not all ants live underground, for example "African weaver ants live in the treetops whereas tiny trapjaw ants live in small colonies inside split twigs". (lines 9–10)
15.	C	Their long tongues allow them to "reach deep into the nests" where the ants are. (line 40)
16.	B	A "predator" is an animal that preys on (eats) other animals.
17.	C	"Regurgitate" means that the ants vomit back up some of the food they have eaten to feed the other ants.
18.	D	"Care" is a verb because it describes what the female ants do for the eggs.

Answers

19.	B	The queen ant has a larger abdomen because that is where the eggs are produced.
20.	D	"Some people in the Philippines and Australia enjoy snacking on ants".

Super Statistics (page 91)

1.	The number of legs ants have.
2.	The number of ant species.
3.	The number of daughter worker ants the queen can produce over a lifespan.
4.	The numbers of caterpillars a colony of ants can gather in one day.
5.	This is how often the queen can lay her eggs.
6.	The number of ants alive in the world at any one time.

14. Black Beauty: questions (pages 94–96)

Question	Answer	Explanation
1.	C	The young horse, Black Beauty, is narrating the story. He talks about his mother and the other colts and uses the words "I" and "my".
2.	D	In lines 40–44, the mother says that she is only a horse: "I never yet could make out why men are so fond of this sport . . . but we are only horses, and don't know."
3.	A	When an animal pricks their ears, they move them to hear what is going on.
4.	B	A "colt" is a young horse.
5.	A	Line 1 says "Before I was two years old". This means that Black Beauty must have still been 1 year old at the time of the hunt.
6.	B	Lines 35–37: "As for me, I was so astonished that I did not at first see what was going on by the brook; but when I did look there was a sad sight; two fine horses were down, one was struggling in the stream, and the other was groaning on the grass."
7.	B	"Dashing" means to move very quickly. "Dawdling" is the opposite of this as it means to move slowly.
8.	D	March is an early spring month.
9.	A	Line 6 describes how the colt heard the sounds of the hunt and cantered off straight away: "The oldest of the colts raised his head, pricked his ears, and said, "There are the hounds!" and immediately cantered off."
10.	D	The author uses exclamation marks in line 13 to show how loud the noise was: "I never heard such a noise as they made. They did not bark or howl or whine, but kept up a "Yo! Yo, o, o! Yo! Yo, o, o!" at the top of their voices."

Answers

11.	B	He did not feel positively about the hunting because he was in agreement with the other colts when he saw the injured horseman and also the "sad sight" of the horses that had fallen.
12.	C	The word "burst" describes how the dogs were moving and is therefore a verb.
13.	C	"There was no noise now; even the dogs were quiet, and seemed to know that something was wrong." (line 51)
14.	B	They were fond of the sport means that they liked it a lot.
15.	A	It is inferred from the text that the boy fell from his horse when the horse missed the stream. (line 35)
16.	D	"By" is a preposition because it is describing where something is.
17.	C	The dogs were hunting the hare and had lost its scent.
18.	A	"Spoiled" in this context means that the horses get injured during the hunt.
19.	C	"When I did look there was a sad sight; two fine horses were down, one was struggling in the stream, and the other was groaning on the grass." (line 37)
20.	B	Line 7: "My mother and an old riding horse of our master's were also standing near, and seemed to know all about it." This tells you that one of the other horses was a riding horse but the reader is not told about the mother.

Obliging Onomatopoeias (page 97)

1.	sheep
2.	donkey
3.	crow
4.	chicken
5.	deer
6.	frog
7.	lion
8.	pigeon
9.	turkey
10.	grasshopper

15. Deforestation: questions (pages 100–102)

Question	Answer	Explanation
1.	A	"Essential" and "indispensable" are things that you can't do without.
2.	B and D	These are the examples given in the text.
3.	C	"Hot topic" is a saying which means that people have spoken about a subject a lot.

Answers

4.	B	"Graze" is a verb because it describes an action that animals do
5.	C	15% of all emissions result from deforestation and, therefore, 85% do not.
6.	D	50 years = 17–20% so 100 years = 34–40%
7.	D	Diamonds are not mentioned in the text.
8.	C	Line 42: "Wildfire is one of the biggest causes of deforestation. It is natural and, sadly, unavoidable."
9.	B	The author is concerned about the future of the rainforests throughout the text.
10.	A	Repetition of the first letter of each word is alliteration.
11.	B	Farmers need space to grow crops which is explained in lines 25-29.
12.	B	"Indigenous" means native or original.
13.	D	It is an adjective describing the "part" of rainforests.
14.	B	Including figures ensures that readers know the numbers and therefore the impact.
15.	C	The other three options would assist in preventing deforestation.
16.	B	Lines 36-37 explain that many people cut down trees without permission, so we can infer that a permit would allow them to cut trees legally.
17.	D	The tone of the passage is concerned for the state of our rainforests, but it is also informative because it tells readers the facts and figures and also how they can help prevent deforestation.
18.	C	"Not only will future generations be unable to experience the diverse wildlife within the rainforests, but deforestation could have more serious implications for the state of our planet." (lines 8–10)
19.	A	The opposite of "major" is "minor".
20.	D	"In 2014, three hundred and eighty-one new species of animals and plants were discovered in the Amazon Rainforest, which is a truly amazing figure." (lines 13–15)

Grand Glossary (page 103) (Example answers:)

Indigenous	Relating to the people who originally lived in a place.
Ecosystem	Living things in an area, how they affect each other and the environment.
Commodities	Things that can be traded, bought or sold.
Civilisation	The culture/way of life of human society.
Global warming	The gradual increase in world temperatures caused by gases in the air.
Diverse	many different types of people or things.

Answers

Greenhouse gases	Gases that cause the greenhouse effect.
Livestock	Farm animals and birds.
Cosmetics	Substances you put on your face or body such as cream or make-up.
Vapour	Gas or tiny drops of liquid following the heating of a liquid or solid.

16. Forest: questions (pages 105–107)

Question	Answer	Explanation
1.	C	Both words in the phrase "frightening forest" start with the same sound.
2.	A	It is a simile because the word "like" is placed in front rather than making a direct comparison. The branches are compared to witches' fingers.
3.	D	"Wintry" is an adjective which describes the night.
4.	B	He has a wet nose and wagging tail.
5.	C	"Happiness" is an abstract noun; it is a thing that you can't touch.
6.	B	The mood is tense but not petrifying.
7.	D	"After what seemed like a lifetime, Allegra reached the street. She burst out of the frightening forest and into the warm cosy street lighting. Her mood immediately transformed as she felt safe and secure in the street where she had grown up. A few metres down the road she spotted her home." (lines 11–14)
8.	D	The extract starts with "It was a cold wintry night." which is the clue that it is set in a winter month. Also, we are told that "the days got shorter and the nights grew darker" which is another clue.
9.	A	The first paragraph explains that she is uneasy but doesn't say that she hates walking in the forest: "She was accustomed to walking home from school through the woods but, as the days got shorter and the nights grew darker, she felt less comfortable doing so."
10.	C	Line 11 tells us: "After what seemed like a lifetime, Allegra reached the street". Then in line 13, we learn that this is "the street where she had grown up" which indicates that she is home.
11.	B	If things work like clockwork, there is a strict routine and things happen at a certain time.
12.	C	"The whistling of the wind sounded like pitch pipes." (lines 2–3)
13.	A	"Nit-picking" is when someone picks on small details that don't really matter.
14.	B	She is uptight and a perfectionist as the text talks about everything running like clockwork, things being in their own place, nit-picking, and "there was not a speck of dust in sight."
15.	C	"Spontaneous" means without planning.

Answers

16.	C	"She glanced at the clock in the hallway and it showed five-thirty. Dad would be home in half an hour and dinner would be on the table." (lines 26–28)
17.	A	She was concerned at the beginning of the text and then frustrated at her living situation.
18.	A	"Wrath" means "anger" or "fury".
19.	D	"Extreme" is an adjective that describes the weather conditions.
20.	B	The use of the imagery creates a sinister tone because it makes the trees seem as if they are alive and reaching out for Allegra.

Smart Similes (page 108)

1.	fox
2.	lion
3.	bone
4.	owl
5.	angel
6.	whistle
7.	post
8.	peacock

17. Pinocchio: questions (pages 111–113)

Question	Answer	Explanation
1.	C	This is a metaphor: his voice was thunder. A simile would say "His voice was like thunder".
2.	B	Pinocchio was not listening; he continued to make fun of Geppetto and did not change his behaviour even when Geppetto was cross.
3.	C	A Marionette is a puppet.
4.	A	He knew a family all called Pinocchis and so he said "I think I'll call him PINOCCHIO."
5.	D	"After choosing the name for his Marionette, Geppetto set seriously to work to make the hair, the forehead, the eyes." (line 12)
6.	A	Other synonyms for "impertinent" include "rude", "insolent", "impolite", "unmannerly", "ill-mannered", "bad-mannered", "uncivil" and "discourteous".
7.	B	It is an adjective as it describes the trick.
8.	D	Lines 36–37 says that Pinocchio's legs were "so stiff that he could not move them".
9.	C	The police officer "hearing all that noise, thought that it might be a runaway colt". A colt is a young male horse.

Answers

10.	B	"Bravely" is an adverb as it describes the verb "stood".
11.	A	Pinocchio plays tricks on his master before he has even been made by stealing his wig and running away.
12.	D	In this case, the verb "flew" means a swift movement.
13.	C	We know that Pinocchio stuck his tongue out at Geppetto because line 22 says "The mouth stopped laughing, but it stuck out a long tongue."
14.	A	The word "like" is used so it is comparing the two things and is a simile.
15.	C	Pinocchio's nose was so long that it made it easier to catch him: "The Carabineer grabbed him by the nose (it was an extremely long one and seemed made on purpose for that very thing)." (lines 50–51)
16.	A	Almost as soon as Pinocchio was made and started playing tricks Geppetto said: "I should have thought of this before I made him. Now it's too late!"
17.	B	The people were crying because they were laughing so much. "But the people in the street, seeing a wooden Marionette running like the wind, stood still to stare and to laugh until they cried."
18.	A	He was insulted that Pinocchio was staring. Lines 13–15 says: "Fancy his surprise when he noticed that these eyes moved and then stared fixedly at him. Geppetto, seeing this, felt insulted and said in a grieved tone: "Ugly wooden eyes, why do you stare so?""
19.	C	He put the yellow wig on his head "which was half swallowed up in it".
20.	D	The fire and the pot of something bubbling away were only painted on the wall, so any answer option that lists these cannot be correct.

Splendid Synonyms (page 114)

Example answers:

Old	mature, aged, senior
Ugly	unattractive, unpleasant, hideous
Poor	bad, defective, unsatisfactory
Sharp	precise, intense
Stiff	rigid, inflexible, hard
Wide	broad, spacious, vast
Big	huge, enormous, large
Long	lengthy, extended, protracted

Answers

18. Planets: questions (pages 117–119)

Question	Answer	Explanation
1.	D	The text says that the planets are ordered by their distance from the Sun. Mercury is nearest to the Sun while Neptune is the furthest planet from the Sun. (lines 1–3 and 36)
2.	C	They orbit the Sun. (lines 3–5)
3.	C	Colons are used at the start of a list. There is a short list on lines 4–5.
4.	D	"Orbit" means moving in a circle around something – in this case, the Sun.
5.	B	"Sufficient" means enough of something.
6.	D	Mnemonics are used when people are trying to remember something.
7.	C	It is difficult to study due to its proximity to the Sun.
8.	B	Lines 7–8 states that "The Roman Mercury used to carry messages between the gods."
9.	B	The Moon is the brightest object in the sky at night.
10.	A	"Opaque" means cloudy or not able to see through.
11.	A	The scientists have only made speculations about the impact of an asteroid but it is not known for certain.
12.	C	"Mars is a more elongated shape than the other planets which causes extreme seasons owing to its orbital path around the Sun." (lines 21–23)
13.	B	"The inner core of the planet is solid but there are also layers of liquids and gases." (lines 37–38)
14.	A	Galileo was an astronomer as he studied the planets and stars, but he was also a scientist.
15.	C	"It is pale blue in colour and this is caused by the water, ammonia and methane ice crystals that form its upper atmosphere." (lines 34–35)
16.	A	The text states that the storm on Neptune lasted for "around five years" which means "roughly five years". (line 39)
17.	A	"Predominantly" is a synonym for "mainly".
18.	A	"The closest planet to the Sun, and the smallest, is Mercury." (line 6)
19.	A	Line 15 states that Venus "appears to be a cloudy white colour".
20.	A	As stated in line 27, Saturn is "the most distant planet that can be seen by the naked eye from the Earth".

Answers

Memorable Mnemonics (page 120)

Answers will vary as it is your own creation.

19. The Velveteen Rabbit: questions (pages 123–125)

Question	Answer	Explanation
1.	D	The story took place at Christmas, which is in December.
2.	A	The extract discusses how the Velveteen Rabbit can be real.
3.	C	The text explains that the Skin Horse has been around for a long time and knew a lot of things: "The Skin Horse had lived longer in the nursery than any of the others", "He was wise, for he had seem a long succession of mechanical toys arrive to boast and swagger" and "Only those playthings that are told and wise and experienced like the Skin Horse understand all about it". (lines 26–33)
4.	C	The Velveteen Rabbit asked the Skin Horse if he was real after he described real toys as being "shabby".
5.	B	"Carefully" is an adverb to describe how things had to be kept.
6.	A	""Does it hurt?" asked the Rabbit." (line 40)
7.	D	"Substandard" meaning not good enough and "superior" meaning better than average.
8.	B	"Snubbed" means to not pay someone any attention or to ignore someone.
9.	C	"Even Timothy, the jointed wooden lion, who was made by the disabled soldiers, and should have had broader views, put on airs and pretended he was connected with Government." (lines 21–22)
10.	B	It is to emphasise that the person has to truly love the toy for it to become real.
11.	A	Lines 27–28 say that "most of the hairs in his tail had been pulled out to string bead necklaces".
12.	B	Lines 13–14 describe the Rabbit as being "naturally shy and being only made of velveteen, some of the more expensive toys quite snubbed him" so it is likely that he felt quite insecure compared to the other toys.
13.	C	Lines 16–17 explain that the model boat "had lived through two seasons and lost most of his paint".
14.	B	When the Aunts and Uncles came to dinner "there was a great rustling of tissue paper and unwrapping of parcels, and in the excitement of looking at all the new presents the Velveteen Rabbit was forgotten". (lines 8–10)

Answers

15.	C	The other options all name other things that are not edible.
16.	C	The Skin Horse had seen mechanical toys "break their mainspring and pass away". (line 30)
17.	D	""What is REAL?" asked the Rabbit one day, when they were lying side by side near the nursery fender, before Nana came to tidy the room. "Does it mean having things that buzz inside you and a stickout handle?""(lines 34–36)
18.	A	It is implied that the people who wouldn't understand are the ones who don't love you or don't understand why the toys are tatty.
19.	B	"Excitement" is an abstract noun as it is a thing that you can't touch.
20.	D	"His coat was spotted brown and white."

Numerous Nouns (page 126)

Common nouns	Proper nouns	Abstract nouns
table	Thursday	joy
car	Joypreet	fear
metal	Russia	love
clock	Rome	envy
bridge	Berlin	bravery

1.	Orcas
2.	Bees
3.	Lions
4.	Apes
5.	Geese
6.	Monkeys

20. Volcanoes: questions (pages 129–131)

Question	Answer	Explanation
1.	D	Line 7 explains that "extinct volcanoes are unlikely to erupt again".
2.	A	"Maintained" is closest in meaning to "preserved".
3.	C	"Drizzle" implies that the lava is falling down lightly.
4.	C	Line 19 gives the order of the four phases and Strombolian is the second phase which "involves thicker lava and some mild explosions".
5.	B	Line 33 explains that the uncovered bodies would show what life had been like on the morning of the eruption in AD79.

Answers

6.	C	"The soil surrounding volcanoes is extremely fertile and is perfect for growing crops and plants." (lines 43–44)
7.	D	Lines 10–11 state that the plates move "as a result of the pressure from the heat energy that comes from the centre of the planet".
8.	B	The definition of a reservoir is "a large natural or artificial lake used as a source of water supply". The magma collects in a reservoir until the pressure forces it up.
9.	A	"The Peleean phase involves fine ash, thick lava and gas-charged clouds which travel downhill at tremendous speeds." (lines 24-25)
10.	C	Line 24 describes the magma as "almost solid".
11.	B	"Concealed" means to be hidden which is opposite in meaning to "uncovered".
12.	D	Safety valves are put in place to release pressure in objects such as boilers. The same applies to volcanoes.
13.	C	This is inferred: as the plate is pushed down to the centre of the Earth, the rock melts which suggests that the centre of the Earth is very hot.
14.	B	The word "tragic" is a synonym for "disastrous".
15.	D	Lines 15–17 explain that "magma is forced up through the Earth's crust" and comes from the centre of the Earth.
16.	C	The text states that Vesuvius is famous in European history.
17.	C	"Produce" can be both a verb and a noun but, in this sentence, it is a verb because it is a process to make hot water.
18.	D	The ash reducing the temperature worldwide is stated as the cause of the crops failing: "The ash that gathered in the atmosphere as a result of this eruption reduced the temperature worldwide and 1816 became known as "the year without summer". The death toll was much higher than the original 92,000 owing to the lack of summer and to crop failures since crops as far away as Europe and America were affected." (lines 36–40)
19.	D	"Devastating" and "natural" are both adjectives, while the other answer options contain other word types.
20.	A	"Tremendous" is the adjective to describe the speed at which the lava was moving.

Popular Prepositions (page 132)

1.	on
2.	above
3.	for
4.	on
5.	at

Marking Chart

Fill in the tables below with your results from each test. Each test is out of 20 with a total of 100 questions in each section below.

Comprehensions

	Test 1	Test 2	Test 3	Test 4	Test 5	Total
Score	/20	/20	/20	/20	/20	/100

	Test 6	Test 7	Test 8	Test 9	Test 10	Total
Score	/20	/20	/20	/20	/20	/100

	Test 11	Test 12	Test 13	Test 14	Test 15	Total
Score	/20	/20	/20	/20	/20	/100

	Test 16	Test 17	Test 18	Test 19	Test 20	Total
Score	/20	/20	/20	/20	/20	/100

Progress Grid

Colour the chart below with your percentage mark from each comprehension test to see how well you have done.

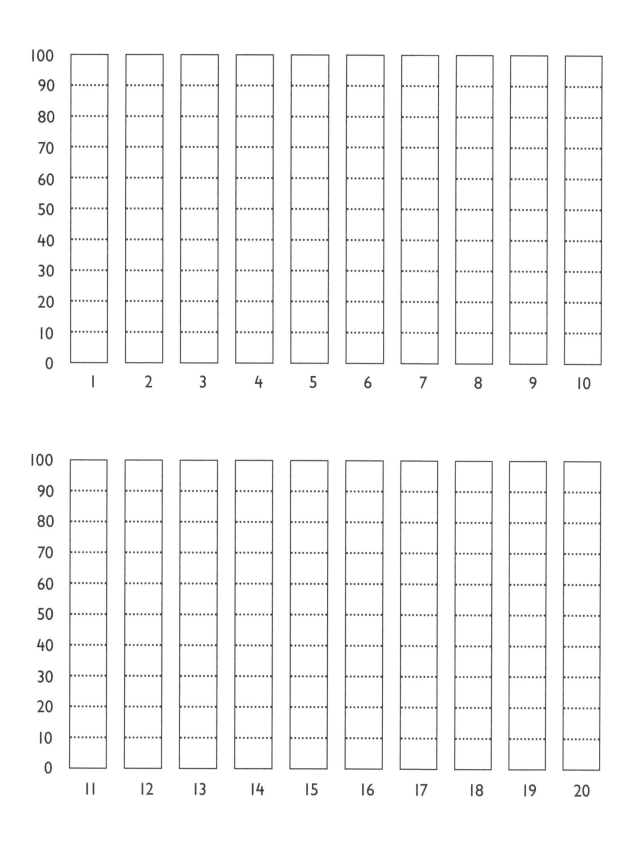

Progress Grid

Read the statements below for some hints and tips.

Below 30%   Remember to read the passage thoroughly to ensure it makes sense.
             Retry the passages and continue to build your vocabulary.

31% to 50%   Read ahead of the gaps to help with the contextual clues.

51% to 70%   Good effort. Continue to build your vocabulary by learning word definitions
             and synonyms.

71% to 90%   Well done. Keep enhancing your word knowledge.

91% +   You're a Comprehensions star. Keep up the hard work.

THIS PAGE HAS DELIBERATELY BEEN LEFT BLANK

**THIS PAGE HAS DELIBERATELY
BEEN LEFT BLANK**